HIGHER EDUCATION
AS A FIELD OF STUDY

The Emergence of a Profession

Paul L. Dressel
Lewis B. Mayhew

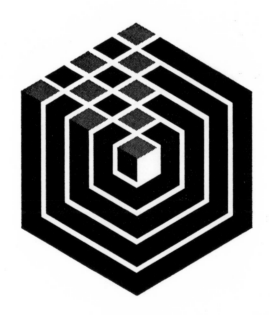

HIGHER EDUCATION AS A FIELD OF STUDY

Jossey-Bass Publishers

San Francisco · Washington · London · 1974

378.00711
D773 h
1974

HIGHER EDUCATION AS A FIELD OF STUDY
The Emergence of a Profession
by Paul L. Dressel and Lewis B. Mayhew

Library of Congress Catalogue Card Number LC 73-21073

International Standard Book Number ISBN 0-87589-226-4

Manufactured in the United States of America

JACKET DESIGN BY WILLI BAUM

FIRST EDITION

Code 7419

The Jossey-Bass

Series in Higher Education

PREFACE

*H*igher education as a field of study well characterizes our principal interests since the late forties. After extensive collaboration for several years at Michigan State University, our ways parted. Our respective approaches to the study of higher education have also shifted both in focus and in method, as will be amply apparent to the sensitive reader.

We initiated this book with no certainty as to the extent of our agreement about the higher education scene or the need for higher degree programs in this field. Hence we developed our outline so that we could work essentially independently and determine the extent of our agreement or disagreement as work proceeded.

Chapter One, a review of the study of higher education and its literature, provides a natural starting point for any analysis of higher education as a scholarly field.

Chapter Two presents the most complete picture and analysis of programs on higher education available to date and describes one representative higher education program in detail.

Chapter Three discusses the various components of current programs; the role of research and the value of a thorough grounding in research techniques for all degree candidates; plus the type of training which has proven most beneficial.

Chapter Four highlights the complexities, problems, and issues in higher education as a field of study as well as those of the programs themselves. Included are views of recent graduates as well as our own assessments of shortcomings.

Chapter Five presents our recommendations for how programs might be altered to better serve the needs of degree candidates and of higher education generally.

Chapter Six presents a typology and a series of observations and principles which we believe will be useful to those who wish either to review and revise existing programs or possibly to develop new (and we suspect unneeded) ones.

Some readers will surely be disappointed that we have not taken a more rigorous position on the essential characteristics of programs and the desirability of altering or eliminating many of the existing ones. However, we regard higher education programs as still being in a developmental stage. We believe that while the number of programs and the number of candidates are admittedly excessive in reference to current and future needs, this oversupply in itself may be the most potent factor in bringing about a focus on quality and an adjustment between supply and demand.

Professors and students in many programs indicate that they are ready for critical review—indeed, such reviews are already in process on some campuses. We hope that *Higher Education as a Field of Study* will both stimulate and be useful in such review. For ourselves, we have enjoyed and benefited from collaboration in this effort and have been gratified to find ourselves in essential agreement on most if not all points.

We express our appreciation to those who have been helpful in this project. The many professors, degree recipients, and administrators who responded to our requests for information and materials have certainly earned our gratitude. Marion M. Jennette, who typed several drafts, prepared final copy, and assumed responsibility for checking and preparing the Bibliography, was essential to the completion of the task. Sheila J. Hoeve was most helpful in the early stages of collection and ordering of the copious materials on which Chapter Two is based. As usual, Ruth A. Frye assisted in many ways and at crucial points.

East Lansing, Michigan   Paul L. Dressel
Stanford, California   Lewis B. Mayhew
July 1974

CONTENTS

HIGHER EDUCATION
AS A FIELD OF STUDY

The Emergence of a Profession

Chapter One

EMERGENCE OF THE FIELD

*A*lthough the study of higher education has yet to reach maturity, it possesses many of the attributes of a scholarly field. Programs designed to prepare persons for entry into professional work in higher education exist in profusion. There are approximately eight hundred professors who think of themselves as professors of higher education. Departments of higher education and centers or institutes affiliated with universities sponsor research concerning higher education as well as provide degree and public service programs. A growing literature deals with various parts of the higher education domain. And a growing bureaucracy associated with quasieducational organizations concerns itself with generating new and systematic knowledge about higher education. Indeed, one of the serious problems in trying to view higher education as an entity is the plethora of individuals and organizations producing relevant materials and the extensive range of reports and studies which bear directly on understanding higher education. Individuals can begin professional work or scholarship in higher education from any of a multiplicity of formal academic preparations, and the contributing disciplines are so numerous and extensive as

1

to preclude any emergent transcending and interpreting theory. Hence, higher education as a field lacks some of those critical unifying attributes of other professions and historical scholarly fields. Yet professors, administrators, agency and secretariat workers, and the professional staff members of testing programs, regional compacts and consortia, who regularly attend such conferences as the annual National Conference on Higher Education, feel an affinity for each other and identify with an intuited concept of higher education as a set of problems requiring scholarly study.

Field of Study or Discipline?

Any attempt to discuss higher education as a field of study leads to speculation about the precise meaning of *higher education*. As a field of study in colleges of education, higher education followed the creation of programs of elementary and secondary education for the preparation of school teachers, but unlike them, higher education units became the repository of courses and experiences not only for teachers throughout postsecondary education but also for administrators, researchers, and public service personnel in technical institutes and community colleges; adult, continuing education, or lifelong education programs; liberal arts colleges; graduate schools; professional schools; and universities; and for federal, state, and regional organizations involved in financing and coordinating these institutions. Today, as we define it, higher education as a field of study includes research, service, and formally organized programs of instruction on postsecondary education leading to a master's degree, educational specialist or other two-year certificate or degree, or doctorate whether oriented toward teaching, service, institutional research, or scholarship.

Some universities include as higher education features that are not encompassed in this definition—for example, courses in higher education offered to graduate students and occasionally even to undergraduates but not formalized as degree programs. Thus preparation in disciplinary-based Ph.D. programs for teaching the traditional disciplines in colleges and universities is not included in this definition and not emphasized in this book, despite its importance, whereas preparation for undergraduate instruction, most commonly in the community colleges, through the doctorate in higher education is included.

With higher education clearly a field of study in this sense, is it a discipline as well? The concept of a discipline probably is one of the most overworked and ill-defined terms bandied about in the academy. Yet the attempt to analyze higher education as a discipline may be helpful in comparing the characteristics of this relatively new and amorphous specialty with those subjects which have evolved into reasonably distinctive fields of study and scholarly activity.

One commonly accepted criterion of a discipline is a general body of knowledge which can at least be forced into some reasonably logical taxonomy, so that scholars can tell, at least quantitatively, where gaps in accepted knowledge exist. The growing body of literature concerning higher education provides more knowledge of the opinions of writers, however, than knowledge of the phenomenon of higher education. Its taxonomies or classification systems are rudimentary and currently not sequentially ordered. Subsumed under each of the rubrics are few mutually exclusive subordinate classifications: pursuit of any one rubric in depth leads to concepts used in other rubrics.

A corollary of this first criterion is that a discipline should possess both a specialized vocabulary and a generally accepted basic literature, which at least outlines its parameters. Higher education is in a paradoxical position with respect to these conditions. Words and phrases such as *general education, statewide coordination, governance, collegial, departmental* or *board-of-trustee prerogatives* are used by specialists in higher education in somewhat precise ways, but descriptively rather than analytically. Certain books and articles are found on most bibliographies for courses dealing with higher education, with the names of M. M. Chambers, Robert M. Hutchins, Clark Kerr, David Riesman, and John Dale Russell, associated with generally recognized works. However, that literature generally does not define the field, nor are there texts which even purport to indicate basic principles in the sense that a basic text in physics or sociology does.

Moreover a discipline commonly involves some generally accepted body of theory and some generally understood techniques for theory testing and revision. Here the literature of higher education appears decidedly lacking. There are, of course, theoretical notions concerning developmental needs of college youth as advanced by such scholars as Kenneth Keniston, Nevitt Sanford, and Joseph Katz; and other researchers such as J. Victor Baldridge and James G. March have sought to apply organizational theory to understanding how colleges and universities function. But for the most part, writing and experimentation in higher education thus far rests on theoretical considerations idiosyncratic to a given individual or other fields of study—a phenomenon which virtually precludes systematic theory-building and testing.

Presumably another essential of a discipline is a generally accepted body of consistently applied techniques of analysis or a generally agreed-upon methodology. The literature of relatively precise disciplines such as mathematics, physics, chemistry, and increasingly, experimental psychology, is almost stylized, so well understood are their analytical tools. Partly because higher education embraces such a multiplicity of phenomena and partly because those who study it represent a variety of academic backgrounds, a commonly understood methodology of inquiry just does not exist. Hence scholarship based on a systematic research strategy must communicate that strategy in detail, or (as is true with perhaps the bulk of the writing) let research strategy remain implicit and covert. The scholarly technique most typically used in the study of higher education is for an individual to observe a phenomenon—the presidency, boards of trustees, access to higher education or whatever—using quite idiosyncratic methods of collecting comparative data and all too frequently generalizing in a highly personal way.

Related to and perhaps inseparable from these criteria is that of recognized techniques for replication and revalidation of research and scholarship. In a few components of the presumed domain of higher education such replication is possible, although scarcely with the accuracy or control of field crop or feeding experiments. For example, Wilbert J. McKeachie has replicated studies on the effectiveness of college teaching; studies of the backgrounds of scientists and scholars have been reexamined using the same data but treating them differently; and literally thousands of studies have tested indices predictive of college achievement. But for the most part, research and scholarship focusing on higher education have not been and probably can not be replicated. Consider, for example, the highly important subject of statewide coordination and control of higher education. During the late 1960s, five or six scholars operating independently studied this phenomenon and reported their results. While the findings can be compared at a somewhat superficial level, the research strategies were so personalized as to defy replication. In addition, the original efforts were sufficiently expensive as to make replication questionable in view of the value and utility of the additional findings.

As scholarly fields mature and gain acceptance, they acquire trappings which symbolize their status as disciplines—scholarly associations restricted to those with at least rudimentary competence in the field; journals using referees to screen materials submitted for publication for evidence of competent scholarship; mutual recognition of more and less competent scholars, with those judged the more able regularly called upon to judge the others. Here higher education as an evolving field again reveals its youth. Associations concerned with the broad field of higher education, in contrast with the disciplinary and professional associations, are either associations of institutions and organizations such as the American Council on Education, whose leadership and voting constituency consists of administrators from institutions and other associations, or associations of individuals such as the American Association for Higher Education, which requires only an interest in the subject for membership. Although the relevant journals (for example, the *Journal of Higher Education, College and University,* the *Educational Record,* or *Liberal Education*) certainly seek quality in the materials published, they do not utilize the rigorous refereeing procedures employed in other fields. And while there are individuals of accepted stature who write or conduct research in higher education, they may not occupy leadership roles in relevant associations and may seldom be involved in judging research proposals or research results of others.

Most disciplines have a recognized sequence of experiences for the preparation of scholars and research workers, but no such generally recognized sequences of experiences exist for scholars of higher education. A mature discipline occupies a recognized place in relation to other disciplines and has clearly perceivable linkages to them; but although there are some relationships between higher edu-

cation and other fields, especially in the social and behavioral
sciences, these relationships do not appear to derive from a logic
such as that which relates physiology, comparative anatomy, and
medicine. Nor within the field itself are there clear relationships between governance, learning, finance, or the curriculum. Another
criterion is difficult to apply yet of some significance: from a disciplinary standpoint, research is frequently dichotomized as basic or
applied, and scholars in a mature discipline devote considerable
energy to solving basic or theoretical questions. In higher education
virtually all current research and scholarship must be labeled applied. Relatively little effort is directed to theory building and virtually none is comparable to biochemical research, in terms of fundamental understanding of the field.

But of all criteria of a discipline, possibly the key is a sense
of sequence which enables scholars to predict where they should look
next. The simplest example is, of course, the periodic table which
enabled chemists to know what new elements should be sought. The
field of higher education possesses no such elegance. No compelling
logic tells a scholar that the next step after a study of academic
governance is a study of unionism as opposed to a study of legal
interpretations of higher education, a study of tenure, or a review of
the curriculum.

It is true, of course, that knowledge of the established and
recognized parameters of a discipline may restrict creative scholarship, especially if those parameters preclude linkages with other disciplines. Still, a discipline with stable outer limits helps define the
importance of issues in one field as contrasted to another. This is an
especially vexing problem for an emerging field concerned with a
complex variety of phenomenon. For example, should scholars of
higher education concern themselves with educational programs
offered by churches, businesses, and labor unions? Should they be
concerned with budgeting procedures as much as with structures of
governance? Should the field be expanded to include computer programming for simulation planning models for collegiate institutions?
Because planning for higher education must be done in the context
of broad patterns of social change should futurists such as Alvin
Toffler be assumed to be essential in the domain? This particular
issue of boundaries and focus has considerable staffing implications

for programs in higher education. A school of medicine would be judged deficient if it lacked specialized strength in internal medicine, surgery, and pathology. But while junior colleges and adult education programs are numerically large enterprises within higher education, would a department of higher education be deficient if it did not offer work specifically concerned with those two areas?

Higher education thus appears to be a field of study—ill-defined at the parameters—that is potentially useful in understanding many phenomenon and in preparing people for careers in higher education. But if the criteria suggested above are valid in defining a discipline, higher education has not yet attained that distinction.

Origins of Field

Numerous strands and episodes are contributing differently to the emergence of higher education as a field of study. Historically first were the institutional histories, such as *The College of William and Mary* (1887) by Herbert Baxter Adams, *The Influence of Reconstruction: Education in the South* (1913), by Edgar W. Knight, and the several volumes of *The Tercentennial History of Harvard* by Samuel E. Morison, published during the 1930s. While their quality and value have varied enormously over the generations, these studies have furthered the belief that educational institutions and processes can be understood through the application of scholarly techniques. In a similar vein, descriptive evaluative and analytical studies, such as those of Abraham Flexner concerning medical education and the American university, were premised in the belief that scholarly examination of a complex educational phenomenon could provide a basis for policy formulation. G. Stanley Hall held this attitude in his studies at Clark University, where he offered the reputedly first course on higher education in 1893 (Burnett, 1972). A similar belief undergirded work at the University of Chicago during the 1920s and 1930s when such men as Floyd W. Reeves, A. J. Brumbaugh, and John Dale Russell examined various higher education institutional practices as a basis for establishing principles of administration or finance.

Closely associated ideologically with these activities was the evolution of institutional research as a way of better understanding how individual institutions function. W. H. Cowley (1959) has identified early nineteenth century activities which could be classed as institutional research, but modern research is really more of a twentieth century phenomenon. W. W. Charters developed the concept at Ohio State University; reinterpreted it at Stephens College at Columbia, Missouri; and asserted the principle that institutional research was a continuing and essential internal audit of the educational program of a collegiate institution. During earlier and slower times, institutions had functioned with quite primitive data, particularly since some persons could carry in their heads for a long period of time a supply of data and history sufficient for the decisions to be made. But as budgets and enrollments expanded and turnover of personnel increased, an informal institutional memory no longer sufficed; and more institutions created offices of institutional research. It readily became apparent that specialized training would be necessary if adequate institutional research were to be conducted, and so these offices turned to major universities both for preservice and inservice training of individuals for this research role. At the same time a generalized expectation arose that at least some universities would develop sophisticated techniques of research for use in examining higher education at large. Thus the expansion of offices of institutional research has provided both direction for the study of higher education and empirical evidence upon which some of its generalizations could be based.

Closely related to the emerging concept of institutional research was the expanding interest of institutions in making self-studies. The impetus seems to have derived first from regional accrediting associations and secondly from philanthropic foundation support. During the 1950s, accreditation by a regional association became an essential condition for institutional certification by various state and federal agencies. Hence, many institutions which had previously dismissed accreditation as irrelevant sought it, and found completion of a self-study an essential and usually productive. At about the same time, the regional associations began to require periodic reaccreditation, increasing the volume of self-study. As a prerequisite to making institutional grants, foundations (the Ford Foundation, most notably) frequently sponsored self-studies, such as that at Bowdoin published as *Education In The Conservative Tra-*

dition, or that at Stanford on *The Undergraduate and The University.* The quality of many of these self-studies can best be described as dreary, self-serving, or Utopian, yet their sheer volume produced an introspective attitude among institutions of higher education as well as cadres of individuals who thus learned techniques of institutional analysis.

Another strand, the interrelated evolution of the testing and the counseling and guidance movements, also contributed theory, data and individuals to the field of higher education. The College Entrance Examination Board, organized in 1900, slowly developed into an instrument for articulating secondary and higher educational activities along the eastern seaboard; and with the outbreak of World War II, the Board began to expand its activities to include not only testing but counseling and the curriculum as well. The formation of the Educational Testing Service in 1947 produced what was to become a major center for the study of higher education through psychometric means, and at the same time permitted the Board to extend its research activities into policy formation. The subsequent elaboration of the Iowa Testing Program into The American College Testing Program and the expansion of Educational Testing Service, College Board, and American College Testing Program activities throughout the country during the 1960s produced possibly the three most prolific centers for the generation of information and theory regarding students in higher education. The expansion of testing also included the work of Ralph W. Tyler in developing comprehensive examinations at the University of Chicago; H. H. Remmers at Purdue whose *Studies in Higher Education* included studies of student attitudes; and Lyle Spencer, who adapted psychometric theory to commercially profitable activities in the establishment of *Science Research Associates.*

The testing, counseling, and guidance movements contributed elements of theory, techniques for empirical study, and a substantial cadre of individuals who found their way into the mainstream of the study of higher education. Several national studies each contributed important information as well as people. In the late 1930s, the Progressive Education Association Eight-Year Study and the Cooperative Study of General Education, both under the direction of Ralph W. Tyler, used psychometric devices to appraise educational outcomes, and contributed both to understanding of the lack of articulation between high school programs and college programs and to a clarification of the goals of general education.

Although actually originating earlier, the modern form of counseling and guidance grew directly out of vocational counseling efforts to aid the veterans of World War II. As counseling and guidance centers developed, their professional staffs sought more and more precise information, some of it codified during the 1950s into profiles of American college students, their values and needs. Persons active in the counseling field were the first to attempt theoretical formulations for student behavior, and to provide bases for subsequent research. The differing schools of thought of Carl Rogers and E. G. Williamson produced a substantial body of theory and information which gradually infiltrated other portions of higher education, notably teaching and the curriculum.

In the early 1950s, the Cooperative Study of Evaluation in General Education, under the direction of the authors of this monograph, produced some warrantable assertions about the cognitive gains of college students and enlisted or inducted a substantial number of professors into formal study of higher education. Many of the latter, such as Ruth Churchill at Antioch College, Lily Detchen at Chatham College, Paul Torrance at The University of Minnesota, and William Coffman now at the University of Iowa, subsequently made important contributions to the literature of higher education or to new testing instruments used by other scholars. In addition, the findings of the Cooperative Study became one of the principal bases for Philip Jacobs' *Changing Values in College* (1957), one of the first comprehensive attempts to gauge collegiate impact. The Jacobs study, in a sense, spawned the largest single stream of subsequent research into the impact of college on students.

Another major contributing strand has been the various national or regional commissions which have attempted to provide recommendations or formulate policies for higher education programs and degrees. In 1946, the President's Commission on Higher Education appointed by President Harry S. Truman, building on the earlier *Design for General Education*, demonstrated the under-education of many American students and the need for more detailed study, if the goals of general education for a steadily growing student clientele were to be achieved. The Commission for Financing Higher Education brought together theories about higher education and rudimentary economic theories to present a relatively parsimonious role for the federal government in higher education. The Commission findings were essentially wrong in the light of other social developments; but the volumes of the final report contributed important data and theory not only for finance but for other matters such as faculty personnel. The White House Conference on Education Beyond High School established generalizations concerning the economic plight of the college teaching profession, the likely need for a greatly expanded professoriate, and, in a sense, set the stage for much of the research and theory regarding the academic marketplace which pervaded the nation during the early 1960s.

The Southern Regional Education Board focusing on a single region, was able to demonstrate the serious lag of Southern higher education and the need for more intensive study if the South were to achieve parity with the rest of the nation. Its publication "Within Our Reach," established goals and an agenda for action which made the Southern states one of the more productive sources of research concerning higher education of any region in the nation. These research reports and monographs of the Southern Regional Education Board have been augmented by a substantial volume of institutional research reports from such places as the Florida State University and the Institute of Higher Education at the University of Georgia.

This tradition of commissions culminated in the 1970s in the enormous research productivity of the Carnegie Commission on Higher Education and the polemical focusing on higher educational issues of the Assembly of University Goals and Governance and the Task Force in Higher Education created by the Secretary of Health, Education, and Welfare.

The Carnegie Commission has generated more research about higher education than any other agency in recent times; and the course of its work, reflected in policy statements, reflective essays, and research monographs, almost define the outlines of higher education as a scholarly field. The Assembly on University Goals and Governance, while much less research-oriented, has nonetheless commissioned a number of position papers and has developed policy statements which also help define the field. The much more iconoclastic Task Force on Higher Education, chaired by Frank Newman of Stanford University and composed of people for the most part not formally affiliated with programs of higher education, has taken a critical look at the practices of higher education and has stimulated a great deal of debate about unresolved issues.

In a sense derivative from these national and regional commissions is the strand represented by the many state studies on the state needs in higher education and how they might be met. Some of these studies, of course, were simply political expedients to avoid taking specific actions and contributed little to a scholarly understanding of higher education; but a few not only produced evidence but presented models which would eventually be followed by many other states. California became a pacesetter in this regard as it tried to cope with its staggering expansion. In 1948, George T. Strayer of Columbia University directed a study, *The Survey of the Needs of California in Higher Education,* which gave a reasonably accurate picture of the higher education situation but did not produce any significant policy changes. It was followed by *A Restudy of the Needs of California in Higher Education* under the direction of T. R. McConnell, which amassed an enormous amount of information and organized it so that the public could comprehend how much effort the state would be required to mount. The McConnell study was directly responsible for the creation of the Master Plan for Higher Education, the major elements of which were legislated in 1960. Since the Master Plan, the State of California has been prolific in producing studies and restudies of its higher educational activity, producing volumes of information much of which is generalizable. In a sense a byproduct of the California studies, came the creation in 1956 of the Center for the Study of Higher Education at the University of California, which gathered together a talented group of scholars and contributed much to making higher education as a scholarly field a visible phenomenon. As the California pattern came to be replicated in other states, the volume of reasonably accurate information increased. So did the number of persons involved in those studies who gradually came to think of themselves as professional students of higher education. In addition, the various agencies for control or coordination of higher education produced by these studies have become major employers of graduates of departments and centers of higher education.

The last and most diverse strand in the evolution of higher education as a field of study consists of individuals who, starting from disparate backgrounds, came to think of themselves as professional students of higher education; and who helped define the parameters of a growing field. John Dale Russell, of the University of Chicago program in education, first turned his attention to administration of colleges, then to financial management, and finally to statewide systems of coordination and control. Some of his definitive work remains a standard for reference: his codification of the duties of the Academic Dean is still cited in monographs and administrative handbooks; his conception of optimal institutional size, while somewhat smaller than current estimates, pointed to a continuing valid mode of analysis; and his pattern of conducting statewide studies or surveys which he developed with A. J. Brumbaugh, are still substantially followed.

W. H. Cowley after taking a Ph. D. in Psychology and serving in the Bureau of Educational Research at Ohio State University and, for a time, president of Hamilton College, went to Stanford as a professor of higher education. He worked diligently for 25 years seeking to understand the total field, striving to develop a taxonomy which could aid other scholars of higher education, and in the process developed some of the most insightful historical materials available on higher education and its governance. Several of his students such as Donald T. Williams and E. D. Duryea have carried on parts of his scholarly tradition and are contributing significantly during the 1970s.

T. R. McConnell, coming out of psychology and administrative experience, formed, with Carnegie Corporation assistance, the Center for the Study of Higher Education at the University of California, Berkeley, and focused his attention largely on the public sector and especially on problems of diversity, governance, and control. As the center expanded and became in time the federally supported Center for Research and Development in Higher Education, it concerned itself, among a wide range of projects, with public community colleges and with ways by which students change as a result of the college years.

At the University of Michigan, Algo Henderson, with a background in Public Administration and as president of Antioch College, developed another center for the Study of Higher Education which sought to bridge the gap between professional education and other elements of the University by stressing postdoctoral programs for people trained in disciplines who wished to enter college administration and emphasizing the possibility of improving college teaching through specific research and instruction. Also at the University of Michigan, Theodore M. Newcomb established models for studying the impact of college and for converting research results into policy decisions, and Wilbert J. McKeachie devoted his attention to research leading to the improvement of college teaching—work seminal to efforts at improvement which characterize higher education during the 1970s.

A third center was created at Teachers College, Columbia University, again with Carnegie Corporation support, by Earl J. McGrath, one of the few original scholars in higher education still actively producing (his doctoral dissertation dealt with a subject within the domain). After an administrative career as dean, president and U. S. Commissioner of Education, McGrath joined Teachers College, developed his Institute of Higher Education and focused his energies on studying and understanding liberal arts education, liberal arts colleges, and the dynamics of a liberal arts curriculum. The almost forty monographs produced by the institute under his leadership are probably those most frequently cited in writings about privately supported colleges. McGrath also contributed substantially to another principal focus in the study of higher education, the general education movement; and in 1973 the subject still concerns him as he seeks more rigorously to define the field for analysis.

M. M. Chambers and John Millett have each added dimensions to the field. Chambers, focusing on the courts and higher education, financing of higher education by the states, and on state and national policy formation, has produced a steady stream of monographs and reports which serve as basic data. Millett, after dealing with financing, turned his attention to problems of governance and has contributed a rich vein of thoughtful analyses of the subject based more on clinical experience than on empirical surveys. John

Corson should also be mentioned, for while he has not contributed a large volume of literature to higher education (indeed, he considers himself more a student of public administration), his volume, *Governance of Colleges and Universities* (1960), not only contributed a phrase but a mode of analyzing structures of administration and governance. Corson did for the individual campus substantially what Lyman Glenny did for state systems of higher education with *Autonomy of Public Colleges* (1959), producing the original study and indicating the directions that subsequent scholarship would be likely to take.

Additional names should be mentioned: Nevitt Sanford and his associates showed how developmental psychology could contribute to an understanding of how higher education indeed functions. Harold Taylor, in his more seminal work, demonstrated the relevance of a philosophic tradition not only for understanding higher education but for providing a solid base for educational decision. Taylor demonstrates the freshness and significance of the instrumentalism of John Dewey for collegiate education and—during the 1960s—helped people to understand some of the dynamics of the student protest movement. Cyril O. Houle elaborated the dimensions of adult and continuing education as an essential part of higher education; and Leland Medsker demonstrated that the public junior college could be studied analytically with minimum recourse to hyperbole and polemics. Both Bernard Berelson and Oliver Carmichael dealt with graduate education and set the stage for a great deal of research during the 1960s and early 1970s; and, more recently, Clark Kerr, whose background was labor economics and the presidency of the University of California, has emerged as the major stimulator of research in higher education, as well as a synthesizer of research into policy formulations. Seymour Harris was one of the first recognized and ranking economists to turn his attention to the economics of higher education, thereby establishing a tradition which, by the early 1970s, had begun to flourish and attract the attention of younger economists. David Riesman, with a background in law and sociology, set models for interpretation of higher education, combining historical and sociological data into reflective analysis. Henry Chauncey, as president of the Educational Testing Service, insisted that that agency maintain a vigorous research component and that, further, the ETS should help train research workers. Such a list could, of course, be extended, but these men seem to have identified in their work the major areas of concern to scholars. Much of their work provides data for the more philosophic critics of higher education, such as Jacques Barzun, Alvin C. Eurich, Paul Woodring or Henry David Aiken.

Contributing Forces

A number of forces and conditions in the late 1950s and 1960s called for an even fuller understanding of higher education and more people moving into it in professional capacities. Among them was the rapid expansion of higher education in the United States during the post-World War II period. Enrollments of all sorts increased from approximately 1.5 million students in 1945 to 9 million in 1973 with projections calling for still more increase, to between 11.5 million and 12 million by 1980. During the 1960s alone, enrollments more than doubled, outputs of high-cost Ph.D.'s tripled, remedial work and student financial aids had to be increased, and major new programs were added, such as ethnic studies, urban studies, ecology, and computers. The rapid expansion was accompanied by an even more rapid increase in cost. Higher education required less than 1 percent of the gross national product in 1971–1972 but was expected to account for 3 percent by 1980.

The rapid increases in enrollment and in cost stimulated institutions, as well as state and federal government, to study higher education intensively to determine if large numbers of students could be handled more economically. The more heterogeneous groups of students contributing to the high enrollment required new institutions and programs, adding an ill-understood complexity to the higher educational profile. Before World War II, American higher education consisted of state universities, private universities, single-purpose liberal arts colleges, teachers colleges and normal schools, private and public junior colleges, and a few technical institutes. As the demand for higher education increased, new junior colleges had to be created, branches of existing universities established, and teachers colleges transformed into multipurpose institutions; and the prevailing model of an American institution as a single campus responsible to a president who in turn was responsible to a board of trustees gave way to statewide systems of coordinated campuses, all designed to provide for differentiation of function to serve the increasingly heterogeneous student body. A significant ingredient in this expansion of complexity was the very rapid growth of graduate education and systematic entry of institutions into major research activities. Much of this expansion took place without definite plan or rationale and, well before the middle of the 1960s, it became apparent that adding complexity to a relatively simple administrative and organizational base would invite serious trouble if greater understanding were not developed quickly so that new arrangements could be contrived. Thus the professional study of higher education burgeoned in an attempt to solve problems through providing reasonably definite information, appropriate models, and knowledgeable individuals specifically trained in matters of growth, expansion, and quality.

In more stable days, college administrators had been self-selected through an informal system of identification and on-the-job training. A young faculty member, finding himself on committees and enjoying such work, might quickly move to committee chairmanships and to various sorts of quasiadministrative responsibilities and administrative posts. But when expansion struck, this older, slower system broke down. The need for administrators transcended the ability of the system to produce them informally; faculty mobility increased so that the young faculty member did not stay on a single campus for this socialization to take place; and as administrative problems became more complex, specialization was needed which the earlier informal procedures did not provide. To these deficiencies was added the problem of finding administrators for newly created institutions, particularly public junior colleges. During the peak of their expansion, one new campus was being created each week requiring a full complement of administrative officers. The previous source for junior college administrators—public school administration—was simply inadequate to supply the need, especially since public school systems were expanding at the same time. Thus universities began programs in higher education designed to prepare administrators, especially for the junior colleges. In 1908–1909, Dean James had offered a course on organization of higher education at the University of Minnesota; and by 1920 programs for the professional preparation of college administrators were being offered by the University of Chicago, Ohio State University, and Teachers College. By 1963, eighty-seven institutions were offering some 560 courses in the field (Ewing and Stickler, 1964, p. 401), and higher education programs were increasing at the rate of three to five per year (Ewing, 1963). Foundation and federal support assisted in this effort as in the Kellogg Foundation support of ten junior college leadership programs. Additionally, various internship programs were created; for example, the North Central Association program to produce examiners and consultants, and the Phillips Foundation and, later, American Council on Education program to draft young scholars and prepare them as college or university administrators. Some universities made attempts to provide some specialized training for their own young administrators, and from a few, such as at Syracuse, grew formal programs in higher education. The expansion of all these training programs in the late 1950s and early 1960s brought a collateral need for training materials, including textbooks, case studies, and research reports.

Another stimulus was the demand for more precise planning of higher education and for individuals technically competent and thoroughly familiar with the complexities of the collegiate situation, who could carry out planning activities. In the 1950s when Sidney Tickton was preparing his provocative booklet, *Needed: A Ten-Year College Budget,* not more than a handful of people possessed the economic and analytical skills necessary for the kind of planning Tickton had in mind. Not until afterward did the National Society for College and University Planners come into existence to facilitate exchange of information and, if possible, to inform universities developing programs of the kinds of specialties needed.

During the early 1960s, institutions and systems were faced with requirements for great expansions of budget and physical facilities; and later in the same decade they were faced with requirements to curtail expenditures and to prepare to exist in a stable environment. Both of these situations required much greater knowledge concerning the financing of higher education and the utilization of facilities than available personnel had at their command. Once again universities were asked to produce the economists, business managers, and specialists on space utilization who could serve in the relevant administrative and staff roles; and institutions responded by adding work on the finance or economics of higher education to their curricula as they attempted to provide the needed specialists. Whereas at the beginning of the 1960s, only two economists—Seymour Harris and Sidney Tickton—were devoting much time to the study of higher educational problems, by 1970 a substantial number of younger economists were engaged in significant research and development of material on the financing of higher education. Similarly, state systems and state coordinating agencies for higher education required research and policy-making personnel to interpret higher education to political leaders. As the federal government became more significant in the conduct of higher education, the number and size of Washington-based associations grew dramatically, and each required specialists in higher education research and policy studies. The larger philanthropic foundations came to need large professional staffs with broad understanding of higher education generally as well as specific competencies. Accrediting agencies expanded their functions from the relatively straightforward task of determining if institutions met minimal standards to programs of inservice training of administrators and faculty, developing guidelines for specific program development, and generating data which institutions in their regions could use. All these activities required people who were in short supply. The most frequent solution was, of course, to recruit individuals from various parts of higher education and equip them for the new tasks through inservice experiences. But more specific and relevant preparation seemed appropriate and could, theoretically at least, be provided by university-based programs in higher education.

A particularly vexing problem emerged when the quality of college teaching was assessed and judged inadequate. There was strong reason to believe that doctoral programs were developing research workers but paying little attention to preparing Ph.D. recipients to teach, especially in the undergraduate colleges. Gradually, universities began to experiment with ways of providing Ph.D. candidates with supervised teaching experience and some knowledge of colleges and universities as educational institutions. Thus seminars on college teaching or the nature of late adolescent students began to appear, as did the corresponding need for individuals who could instruct prospective college teachers. Much of the dynamics for the study of higher education at The University of Michigan seems to have been related to this provision of instruction on teaching. In addition to staffing courses on college teaching, that institution also developed a modest demand for individuals who could function in newly created centers for improvement of instruction—staff agencies providing advice and resources to faculty members who wished to improve their own instructional abilities. During their formative period, staffing for these agencies was provided either through drafting outstanding college teachers or those with formal preparation in one of the relevant social or behavioral sciences. However, as their number and size have expanded, the tendency has been to recruit people prepared through formal study of higher education and the demand for such persons seems to be increasing.

Still another factor in the rise of higher education programs is the student protest movements of the late 1960s. Perhaps nothing attracted attention to the problems of higher education as much as these movements did. There had been student protests in the past, but those of the 1960s seemed of a different order of magnitude and a result of much more complicated forces. The phenomenon attracted scholars from psychology, sociology, psychiatry, history, theology, and philosophy as well as those studying higher education. The problem probably stimulated more research, writing, and speculating about the nature of higher education than any other event in recent times; and as compared with scholarly writing about collegiate administration or collegiate financing, the quality and insight appears substantially higher. Some scholars from the disciplines made only brief ventures into the domain of higher education to write a book about the topic; but others such as Seymour Martin Lipset, Kenneth Keniston, Seymour Halleck, and Martin Trow, or Henry David Aiken, who redirected his whole professional interest as a philosopher to examining higher education using philosophic tools of inquiry, became interested and involved and made major time commitments to studying higher education, though they remained administratively outside the field. In addition, campus disturbances stimulated several sustaining research inquiries such as the annual survey of student attitudes conducted by Alexander Astin first at the American Council on Education and now at UCLA.

Another factor stimulating formal academic study and scholarship in higher education was the revolt of minority groups and their demands for full-scale entry into higher education. The efforts of Blacks, Chicanos and Puerto Ricans to develop programs of ethnic studies, modify admissions standards, gain administrative support for minority concerns, and increase financing of minority group education, produced a sharp increase in demand for minority-group administrators. Once again the pool was decidedly deficient. One recourse was to train people on the job; but in anticipation of increased demand for minority-group leadership, minority-group students began to apply to programs in higher education in large numbers, and programs began to accept them and to make specific provisions for them. The impression persists that this particular aspect of training is likely to continue to grow throughout the next several decades. Along with this enrollment in training programs came an expansion of research into the relation of minority groups to higher education. Thus the historically black institution became a focus for research, as did the adjustment problems of black students in predominantly white institutions and how well or poorly the various educational opportunity programs were performing. A previously little-explored facet of American higher education thus quickly became a major dimension of higher education as a field of study.

As have other fields of study, higher education began to flourish in response to the prime nutrient of research—money. Earl McGrath's institute at Columbia and T. R. McConnell's Center at Berkeley thrived because of success in acquiring external funding from foundations or the federal government. The postdoctoral program at Michigan depended heavily on Carnegie funding and was largely phased out when this support was no longer available. Clark Kerr's six-year Carnegie Commission project would not have been possible except for the support of the Carnegie Corporation. Offices of institutional research became possible as budgets were provided for such efforts and their effectiveness has been directly related to the extent of their funding, often from external as well as internal sources. The National Center on Higher Education Management Systems (NCHEMS) at WICHE has been generously supported from the U. S. Office of Education as well as from other sources to generate better data and planning systems for more effective acquisition and utilization of resources; but the various models and programs flowing out of this effort require both institutional funds and expertise for their application, and these resources are not readily available in these days of tight budgets and stable or decreasing enrollments. The Ford Foundation-supported management studies of Frederick Balderston and his colleagues in the Center for Research in Management Sciences at Berkeley are also useful additions to our knowledge about relations between input and output variables even though they, too, may exceed at the moment the know-how and the funds available for wide application in other universities. The overall expansion of schools of education also has contributed to the development of the field. Some have believed that the study of higher education does not belong in schools of education, yet such schools became a natural focus if only because of their degree-conferring power. As these schools moved beyond the limited areas of school teacher and administrator preparation, they developed new units, including those concerned with student personnel activities; and although some schools never developed a viable design for units in higher education, the larger schools felt underprivileged if they could not establish one.

Last, but nonetheless of significance, has been the expansion of publication outlets so that research studies could be published, thus encouraging people to undertake them. The U. S. Office of Education developed a series on *New Dimensions in Higher Education;* McGraw-Hill and Jossey-Bass began their series in higher education, and the College Entrance Examination Board and other organizations began publishing monographs as outlets for research.

All these forces made possible the expansion of higher education as a field of study because of the underlying widespread belief in the value of higher education and of research on higher education. The period of the late 1950s and early 1960s appears in retrospect to have been almost euphoric in this regard: people expected higher education to be able to solve most vexing social problems and research on it to produce the answers it needed to do so. That bull-market period resulted in the first flowering of higher education as a field of study. Now that the bull market has ended and higher education may be viewed as a declining industry, only time will tell whether the momentum generated then can continue.

Possible Alternatives

The responses of institutions of higher education to these forces were varied and are relatively easy to describe, but before doing so it is instructive to consider the alternatives which were possible but not followed.

The first of these was clearly the possibility for existing disciplines of history, psychology, political science, economics, and the like, to accommodate higher education as a special subset of research problems and for people within the disciplines to devote considerable professional time to the study of collegiate institutions as institutions. There are some who felt, and still feel, that such a development might have been fruitful because of being more solidly based. However, for the most part, professors in the mainstream of the various academic disciplines demonstrated remarkable lack of concern for collegiate institutions as objects of study. Sociologists found primary groups and stratification systems of more interest; historians continued their preoccupation with politics, the military, and regional or local history; psychologists, when they were concerned with education, focused on elementary and secondary education or on pathological behavior. It may be that scholars working within other departments of a university cannot divorce themselves from their personal experience sufficiently to satisfy their own scholarly canons. For example, when Talcott Parsons studied college professors, he ended up being almost biographical, giving the impression that professors everywhere are as he imagines his colleagues at Harvard to be. In any event, orthodox academic departments have proved not to be a receptive home for organized study of higher education.

Another possibility was for the study of higher education to be incorporated completely into schools of education and to occupy positions parallel to those of child growth and development, secondary school administration, and the like. Schools of education appeared frequently interested in that model, but those concerned with major collegiate institutions and those concerned with such things as college teaching believed that too close an affiliation with a school of education would be the kiss of death. Additionally, many people who had become marginal to their own academic discipline as they moved into the study of higher education were not enamored of too close a liaison with schools of education. As it turned out, some rapprochement was essential but not as complete as had earlier made the study of the history of education almost the exclusive province of schools of education rather than departments of history.

Still a third model, which was frequently suggested and even now appeals to one of the authors of this book, was the creation of a separate institute or center administratively responsible to a vice-president academic, a provost, or even a graduate dean. This unit would seek to attract people from many different disciplines to study higher education without loosening their affiliations with their basic departments. T. R. McConnell visualized this model for his Center at the University of California at Berkeley, and W. H. Cowley tried for many years of his tenure at Stanford to create such an entity. Generally, however, the idea did not work. Professors in the various disciplines were unwilling to commit themselves to such an institute; the unit did not have degree-conferring status and hence could not control the programs of graduate students; and most universities were unwilling to provide hard-money support for what was viewed as an ephemeral and a less than essential unit; virtually every attempt to implement the model resulted in a drift toward either an organic affiliation with a school of education or the independent status of a contracting body relying on outside grants for essential financing.

Another alternative for which there was some precedent would have been for a single discipline to become preeminent in the study of higher education, much as psychology redefined educational psychology and became the central discipline for elementary and secondary education. However, not only did none of the orthodox disciplines seem willing to involve itself in higher education, but higher education as a field of study simply seems too large and variegated to preclude the hegemony of a single discipline.

A last alternative would have been for research and scholarship concerning higher education to be associated exclusively with separate specialized training programs such as for community colleges or student personnel. When the Kellogg Foundation began to support work on community colleges, the feeling in some quarters was that such specialized training and research programs might become the norm. However, the field of higher education gravitated toward more general programs, and the specialized mode seems to have been almost completely rejected.

Rather than following any one single monolithic model, universities have adopted eclectic arrangements, varying considerably in these elements. Many institutions created offices of institutional research and long-range planning focused on highly applied management problems of concern to the institution itself but offering some opportunities for broader research and producing a number of reports which have general applicability to educational assessment. When these institutional research and planning offices have been administratively located in a satisfactory way and provided with sustaining financing, they have proven both an important source of scholarship and an important training ground for future researchers. A few institutions created offices of institutional and educational research to engage in other activities beyond those of institutional management, such as contract research. Other institutions created centers or institutes with wider foci. Those at Teachers College, the University of Michigan, and the University of California, Berkeley, varied in their emphases from a broad pattern of sustained and focussed research and preservice training at Teachers College, to inservice training and contract survey activity at Michigan and a mixture of research, and contract projects separated from preservice training at Berkeley. The Institute of Higher Education at the University of Georgia was created originally as an institutional research activity for the Georgia system, but then found itself in broader sorts of research activities and engaged indirectly in preservice training of future scholars. Conversely, the Institute for Higher Education at the University of Toledo has been primarily a service agency, albeit with some training responsibility. A substantial number of universities adopted inservice training in summer workshops involving junior colleges, such as workshops for the improvement of teaching at Oregon State University and workshops for the improvement of curriculum at the University of Michigan, which provided not only needed services to the field, but also a focus for the attention of a cadre of individuals primarily interested in the professional study of higher education. Gradually a number of these institutions began to create professorships of higher education and total departments of higher education were charged with educational and service duties, and, when resources allowed, research responsibilities, in various specialized areas such as student personnel services, the junior college administration, institutional research training, and instruction in college teaching for Ph.D. candidates from other departments.

Finally, some college and university presidents became interested enough in the study of higher education to use their own offices as centers for research and scholarship. Clark Kerr has been the prime exemplar of this approach: while still president of the University of California he employed a number of staff associates to help him produce what many believe was one of the most prophetic books about American higher education of the 1960s, *The Uses of the University* (1963). James Perkins similarly became almost a professional student at Cornell, as did Paul C. Reinert, S.J., at St. Louis University, and more recently Warren Bennis at Cincinnati and Howard Bowen at Claremont.

Extrainstitutional Responses

In addition to these institutional responses, a number of extrainstitutional responses have set the pattern for the field. Quasi-educational agencies and organizations and associations have involved themselves in activities directly comparable to those of institutional programs. Not only have the Southern Regional Education Board, the Western Interstate Commission for Higher Education, and the New England Board of Higher Education sponsored research and offered inservice training programs, but the Education Commission of the States, the American Council on Education, the American Association for Higher Education, the Association of American Colleges, the American Association of University Professors and other national and regional organizations have done the same. State master planning commissions, coordinating commissions, and separately designated select committees have also undertaken a relatively large range of research activities. The major foundations have not limited themselves simply to awarding grants. The Carnegie Corporation created the Carnegie Commission on Higher Education and has now established a permanent Carnegie Council on Policy Studies in Higher Education. The Danforth Foundation has not only made grants to investigate innovation but conducted its own fellowship programs and inservice training workshops and institutes. The Exxon Foundation has published research-based policy documents which can help administrators reach sounder decisions and has supported studies ranging from academic fringe benefits and remuneration of administrators to management information systems.

As interest in the formal professional study of higher education has grown, so has the literature dealing with the subject. While much of the book-length treatment of topics has not been produced by faculty members in the majority of programs in higher education, they and their students have become prime consumers of this literature. As should be expected, the subjects of book-length or monographic treatment in recent years has demonstrated a time lag. Thus in 1964, the year of Berkeley, only four books could be identified which dealt with students. By 1969–1970, books dealing with students were being produced at crescendoing rates, and by 1973 that topic seems to have run its course and the financial plight of higher education, first recognized in 1968–1969, was reflected in a large number of titles. In the early history of the professional study of higher education, relatively few books or monographs were based on systematic research, being for the most part reflections or exhortations. Now, however, while polemical titles continue to appear, also a substantial number of reports possessing a reasonable empirical base are published.

Particularly indicative of the growing significance of higher education as a field of study has been the change in coverage of the subject by the popular press. By the end of the 1960s, *Fortune, Look,* and *Life* had devoted single issues to college problems and *Harper's, The Atlantic, New Republic,* and *Saturday Review* had increased the attention given to the field of higher education.

The daily press also reflected the greater significance of

higher education in the national consciousness and covered educational matters with steadily increasing sophistication. And a significant journalistic effort has been *The Chronicle of Higher Education,* which is attempting to keep the profession immediately informed not only of national developments in American colleges and universities but of the substance of books, reports and conferences as they are released or happen.

A particularly productive and illustrative source of information can best be described as fugutive literature—both mimeograph or offset reports and printed softcover documents distributed to a limited audience by universities, such as the ten-volume *Study of Education at Stanford* and the long range academic plan of Vanderbilt, by organizations such as the American College Testing Program and the College Entrance Examination Board, and by state agencies, including state studies and master plans for higher education which contain some of the most solid descriptive information now available about higher education.

The greatest volume of literature on higher education of both high and low quality continues to be contained in conference proceedings. Several of the more widely distributed and comprehensive of these are the Proceedings from the College and University Self-Study Institutes conducted by the Western Interstate Commission for Higher Education and the Center for Research and Development in Higher Education at Berkeley; but many other proceedings not as widely disseminated are of potentially equal value—for example, Duke University's *Management Information Systems in Higher Education: The State of the Art* (Johnson and Katzenmeyer, 1969), and Regis College's *Guidelines for Jesuit Higher Education* (1969).

An unknown terrain—unknown simply because the dimension and quality have never been carefully assessed—are doctoral theses by students in the growing number of higher education programs. A cursory glance at some of them suggests that many are not particularly useful for broad generalization; but they represent a source which could be systematically useful in the future.

The final parameter which defines this emerging field is the number of organizations, associations, and commissions which focus on the study of higher education. The American Association for

Higher Education (AAHE) has long been a natural rallying point for professors of higher education and others concerned with studying colleges and universities: its annual National Conference on Higher Education has become a major forum for the presentation of research and new ideas, and its publications add a significant contribution to the literature. (This commentary on the evolution of the literature of higher education is derived from Lewis B. Mayhew, *The Literature of Higher Education*, 1971.) AAHE was originally a department of the National Education Association and was paralleled in many states by recently active departments of higher education of state education associations. While these state groups have not been particularly productive of research, their annual conferences have provided a forum for students of higher education and an opportunity for those concerned to enjoy some degree of collegiality.

One offshoot of AAHE is the Association for Institutional Research which began informally and then eventually became independent as it sought to elaborate the subspecialty of institutional research and provide outlets for research studies of various sorts. Much less significant was the Association for General and Liberal Studies which, in some respects, grew out of the Committee on General Education of AAHE. This presumably was to be an organization in which professors from many disciplines could come together and discuss collegiate educational problems. As the organization matured it became more a haven for professors in the dwindling number of formal programs in general education and for some who had assumed roles as professors of higher education. The most recent spinoff has been the incorporation of the Association of Professors of Higher Education as a division of AAHE, following a number of years' discussion as to its desirability. Thus far the Association conducts a one-day annual meeting and has issued a limited number of *News Bulletins* and one set of *Conference Proceedings*. It is currently struggling to discover an appropriate identity, and its future will be determined largely by the rate and direction of expansion of research on higher education. If extramural funding of research diminishes significantly and if most programs in higher education become primarily teaching enterprises, the Association will likely remain primarily an annual forum and opportunity for maintaining collegial relationships. If, however, research and scholarship increase and if some of the larger programs develop greater visibility and are increasingly represented in the Association, the organization could become a strong force in sponsoring and encouraging research and developing guidelines for academic programs in higher education.

A paradoxical element in the study of higher education has been the wide-ranging activities and reports of recent national commissions or committees concerned with higher education, but to which relatively few professors of the subject have contributed. For example, approximately 65 studies came from the Carnegie Commission, but only four or five were prepared by such professors. Nor were professors of higher education heavily represented among those commissioned to prepare position papers for the Assembly on University Goals and Governance. This paradox need not be surprising in view of the relative youth of the subspecialty professors of higher education; yet it should serve as a warning if the field is to become an influential force in the evolution of higher education in the United States. Those who profess the subject should be the most knowledgeable in it, and should be viewed as such. In future commissions, professors of higher education should be much more heavily involved than they have been in the past.

Several additional developments have added both to a defined field of higher education and to confusion regarding the essential nature of the field. First, as institutional leaders became concerned about the quality of college teaching on their campuses, centers for the improvement of instruction have come into being, staffed by people who are professionally concerned with the study of higher education. Yet while faculty members in some of these centers have some formal relationship with a department of higher education, the prevailing pattern is for them to be administratively outside the school of education, pursuing activities parallel but unrelated to formal academic programs in higher education. Second, such organizations as the American Council on Education and the several regional compacts have developed research competency in subjects central to the study of higher education, yet for the most part they have conducted this research quite independently of developments in programs of higher education. If university departments of higher education are to mature, such extrainstitutional activities must be brought into tandem with their own work.

What emerges then is an active, confused field, lacking many of the attributes of a discipline, yet demanding more disciplined effort. Its future is obscure; but if the present lines of development are strengthened and if the many perplexities are resolved, it may join the band of established specialties, such as history, sociology, and medicine, which once were in similar limbo.

Chapter Two

CURRENT SCENE

*F*rom the origins discussed in the previous chapter, three somewhat distinctive types of programs in higher education are developing, each pursuing a reasonable and respectable cluster of objectives and demonstrating different approaches to staffing, funding, and the recruitment of students.

The first type is found in institutions which support a department or concentration in higher education in a quest to seek and maintain a national perspective. Generally, from five to ten faculty members throughout the university give major attention to the study of higher education, even if they are not all administratively lodged in the same unit. At the University of Michigan, the University of California at Los Angeles, and the University of California at Berkeley, a number of fulltime professors are housed in the school of education. At Stanford and other universities, one or two professors are located in the school of education but professors in other departments or divisions also work in the same general domain. These programs usually emphasize doctoral level work although some offer study at the master's level work to students with a particular need, such as foreign students who could be expected to move into leadership in their own country and for whom a master's degree may be ample formal preparation. Consistent with a national perspective, these institutions seek to recruit students from all over the United States and from abroad and similarly seek to place graduates over a widely dispersed geographic region. While younger graduates find early placement in relatively minor positions, the aspirations are to prepare people for upper administrative echelons in collegiate institutions, the higher education bureaucracy, government, or organized philanthropy. The parent universities of these programs support faculty appointment in education on a hard-money base, as contrasted with appointments contingent on extramural funding. Additionally, a substantial number of appointments are initially made at high salaries to well-established scholars in the field. Most existing programs of this type are located in complex institutions willing to marshal a rich variety of scholarly talent for a sustained program. For this to happen it is necessary that individuals holding appointments as professor of higher education be generally regarded the intellectual peers of senior professors in other divisions, departments, and units of the university. It is through mutual regard that such desirable efforts as joint programs between higher education and a school of law, for example, can be mounted and sustained. Senior faculty members at institutions supporting this type of program are found in disproportionately large numbers on various national committees and commissions studying higher education. Examples of this sort of program are found in the University of California at Los Angeles, Stanford University, the University of California at Berkeley, the University of Michigan, Michigan State University, the University of Minnesota, the State University of New York at Buffalo, Teachers College, Columbia University, the Florida State University and the University of Texas.

The second type of program is considerably smaller and considerably more local in the sort of student it intends to serve. Such programs offer formal instruction in higher education to junior administrators at the institution itself, and to teachers and administrators needed to staff junior colleges and other institutions in the immediate vicinity there is usually a small fulltime equivalent faculty, possibly no more than one or two persons, aided by administrators teaching parttime who offer practically-oriented courses in their administrative specialties. The student body includes a large proportion of parttime students who work at nearby intsitutions of higher education. Of necessity the curriculum is likely to be limited and composed of courses oriented toward application. There are neither extensive facilities for nor a great interest in developing strong research competencies through internships, apprenticeships or other didactic use of work experience. Since service to a limited geographical area is the hallmark of this kind of program, the fulltime faculty may be more concerned about intimate contact with nearby institutions than with a national reference group. Consulting activities may be carried on rather intensively, but only with a limited number of institutions and organizations in the region. Identifying programs of this sort is somewhat risky, for a great deal of flux and evolution takes place. However, programs that could be legitimately so classified include those at Arizona State University, University of Washington, Southern Illinois University and the University of Pittsburgh.

A third kind of program possesses a much less formal structure. These programs are quite small, staffed by one or occasionally two faculty members offering courses on higher education or preparation for college teaching, generally taken by future junior college teachers and occasionally by doctoral students in other fields at the parent institution who wish some exposure to techniques and theory of pedagogy. Recently, some of these programs have also begun to offer courses on the nature of higher education as a service to undergraduates interested in eventually returning to the university. Faculty members for this sort of program generally come out of professional education, psychology, or social psychology.

Some institutions offering programs of the first type also maintain institutes or centers for research in higher education. Although there is usually great mingling of professional appointments between these two agencies, institutes and centers differ from departments. A department in higher education is essentially a teaching activity which emphasizes advanced graduate degrees plus faculty research, and scholarship. Centers, on the other hand, emphasize research and development activities and, until recently, were frequently supported by extramural grants and contracts. Departments are almost invariably lodged administratively in schools of education. (This resume of types of programs is based on Lewis B. Mayhew's article, "Programs in Higher Education," which appeared in *Higher Education As A Field of Study*, published by The Association of Professors of Higher Education, Washington, D.C., 1972).

Statistics on the number of these programs, departments, institutes, and centers vary greatly (Overholt, 1967; Currie, 1968; Rogers, 1969), depending on the criteria employed in each survey. But excluding all institutions that offer only courses, minor concentrations, or research opportunities in higher education rather than degree programs; and including only those that offer doctoral degrees in the field, we surveyed approximately 80 universities and received information documenting the existence of the 67 doctoral degree programs listed at the end of this book.

These 67 programs are most likely not the total number in existence as of 1974; but the data gathered from them constitutes the most comprehensive overview of higher education programs yet assembled, and the remainder of this chapter will present analyses of these programs based on this survey.

Program Objectives

Statements of goals, objectives, or purposes for higher education programs are perhaps somewhat more carefully thought out than those of other departments in a university. This cautious statement is a highly subjective judgment, but is supported by an extensive experience in studying program objectives. One might reasonably expect some care and sophistication in statements of objectives for a higher education program since clarity or lack of clarity in purposes, goals, and educational objectives is one of the most prevalent concerns yet one of the most obvious deficiencies in universities and their colleges, schools, and departments. Nevertheless, the point of view adopted by higher education faculties in developing and presenting such statements varies. Faculty, departmental, and even institutional purposes are intermixed and confused with student learning objectives. Whereas carefully thought-out statements of educational objectives to be achieved by degree candidates should be available both to the candidates and to faculty, these are too frequently inadequate, unclear, or entirely lacking. Florida State University accomplishes this by indicating that degree recipients should *be able to work with people,* have a *general knowledge of American higher education, specialized knowledge of one area, be able to do research,* and *qualified to teach in lower-division courses.* This composite statement is commendable, but it raises several questions. Is the ability to work with people an initial criterion for selection, an ability which the program proposes to develop, or simply the trite expression of an ideal? Considering the range of higher education courses offered, *general knowledge* requires some explanation. Is this to be defined solely in terms of course requirements which expose the individual to that general knowledge or in terms of facts, concepts, principles, and values characterizing higher education? The latter course is more fundamental than the former since it permits the direct assessment of general knowledge rather than mere rigid course prescriptions. Knowledge also involves a passive scholarly awareness rather than spirited involvement or action as is implied by an extract from a program statement from the University of California at Berkeley: "Concern for prevalent social and educational problems, and a commitment to broadening the accessibility of higher education to all." The latter statement establishes program goals, but these obviously imply emphases, priorities, and objectives to be attained by degree candidates—notably in the affective domain.

The Florida State University objective of specialized knowledge of one area poses, on careful consideration, a need for clarification of both *specialized* and *area.* Some higher education programs avoid the terms by speaking of broad options such as research and administration. Financial, student personnel, and academic administration are further common differentiations. Is the knowledge specialized because a particular area of higher education is studied both more intensively and more analytically than other areas (perhaps as a preparation for research or teaching in the area), or is it specialized (that is, practitioner-oriented) by attention to the bases for decision-making in such fields as academic administration, admissions, budgeting? This scholarly-versus-practitioner emphasis, implicit in many program objectives, is made explicit in others.

The concern for research capability poses a related issue—

that of defining the character and level of the capability. Is the capability directed to understanding and using research or to doing research? Some programs differentiate between the practitioners and the researcher, sometimes to the extent of using the Ed.D. for the first and Ph.D. for the second. Should this distinction in function, if not in degree, be made more clearly, or is it really, in more than one sense, an academic distinction?

Finally, the objective "qualified to teach in a lower-division course" reflects expediency as much as sound planning. The requirement of a cognate may be viewed either as completion of a block of courses outside education having direct implication for either research or practitioner capability or as an extension of undergraduate or master's work to a level of mastery acceptable for lower-division teaching. Conceivably, these alternatives may coincide. A strong minor or cognate in statistics is useful for research, a good background for administrators using data and research reports, and will usually qualify an individual for teaching introductory courses. A similar case could be made for history, philosophy, economics, or numerous other disciplines. However, opportunities or demands for lower-division teaching may not always coincide with research or practitioner interests, and the selection of a cognate purely on the basis of teaching opportunities threatens to turn the degree in higher education into a D.A. or fragment the program into distinctive components required for specific tasks. It would be unfortunate if the doctorate in higher education were to be widely associated with lower-division teaching, for this would surely derogate the character of the degree in the minds of many administrators and faculty members. We do not object to teaching as an ace-in-the-hole in jobseeking or as an occasional or parttime obligation of an administrator in a community college or liberal arts college. We do feel that preparation for teaching lower-division courses is different in level and in kind from research on higher education, teaching higher education, or applying it as an administrator or consultant. It savors of opportunism, attracting students and claiming to meet needs which could be better met in other ways. This is but one of the points at which higher education programs at times seem to seek to be all things to all people.

The University of Florida goal statement indicates that the

"goal of the Division of Higher Education is to foster growth of students and faculty members who are able to infuse their research, teaching, administration and developmental activities with (1) humanizing ideas and (2) an awareness of the social implications of their decisions and actions." Admirable in intent, the goal certainly must be viewed in some delimited context; the implications for selection may well be greater than for deciding when the degree should be awarded.

Obviously, it is difficult to differentiate among broad program purposes, learning objectives for students, and the functions to be performed. Some higher education programs in their statement of purposes emphasize instruction, research, and service in phrases very similar to those used by state universities and land-grant colleges. A few proudly note that the higher education department or center is close to central administration, is regularly consulted about current problems and requested to carry out survey studies or research on them. Other universities have attempted to separate these several tasks by assigning to a center or institute the tasks of research on higher education, of service to other institutions, or both. Any attempt of a unit primarily instructional in nature to serve university demands for institutional studies will almost certainly—because of the time demands—lead to deterioration of the quality of instruction and of the research in the general field of higher education. Extensive offcampus service poses the same problem. The demands are not entirely incompatible, but a unit that is basically instructional is not likely to be granted the additional resources required to maintain instructional quality if it accepts other obligations that are usually both urgent and time consuming.

Dr. Frank Blackington, director of the Michigan State University Honors College, who visited a number of institutions on behalf of this study, remarked that extensive involvement in numerous projects on and off the campus tends to destroy depth, focus, and quality in the instructional program and associated research. The faculty becomes so busy *doing* and *talking* that these activities are confused with scholarship both in their own minds and in those of their students. The tendency is to involve students extensively in service and survey projects. This is useful to the institutions served but may add little to knowledge and expertise either in the field or in the students.

Roaden and Larimore (1973, pp. 50–65) have dealt with this problem insightfully. As they point out, youth is important for the beginning researcher, but maturity (in mind, appearance, and years) is favored for administrators. High levels in both verbal and quantitative ability are essential for success in research, but apparently less so in administration, although verbal facility, above-average height, and social skill are probably helpful. No one knows just what (or even if) courses have much to do with success in either research or administration, although some research skills are, for most persons, acquired more readily from course work than from self-study. Internships are generally regarded as vital for the training of both researchers and administrators, but the internship experience is rather different. Doctoral students who acquire research facilities may take over major responsibilities for research programs with minimal direction. Administrative interns cannot usually be permitted so much freedom and not infrequently administrative decisions take place under such pressure that the intern can neither know the detail involved nor follow the action. Roaden and Larimore conclude: "Programs for preparing persons to be successful researchers and those preparing persons to be successful administrators are markedly different." In view of the confusion in higher education programs the *are* must be interpreted to mean *should be*.

The statements of goals and learning objectives become more diffuse with variability in the range and level of emphases offered. A master's or specialist degree in some phase of higher education (student personnel work, evaluation, administration of admissions and records) may be meaningful in a community college or even in some subsidiary aspect of the operation of a university. A master's or a specialist degree combining some work in education with a sizable bloc of courses in an undergraduate teaching discipline also has significance for a community and occasionally for small liberal arts colleges. The master's may also have some value as a way to ease out unsuccessful candidates for the doctorate. On the whole, however, it is our impression that subdoctorate programs tend to build up such an instructional load and be so focused on practice that both faculty and students are distracted from the scholarly emphasis and knowledge and respect for research which should characterize even the practitioner doctoral degree recipient.

The Center for Higher Education at the University of Virginia in its *Regulations and Guidelines* (April 1972) recognizes some of these problems in planning instructional programs with different emphases and states specific learning outcomes for each. The Administrative Option states that the student should gain: (1) comprehensive understanding of complex organizations, including the nature and function of goals, the nature and effect of varying structures, and the nature and effects of social, political and economic environments; (2) working knowledge of the concepts of power, authority, influence, leadership, conflict (and the tactics and strategies for dealing with it), pluralist social and political theory; (3) special knowledge of college and universities as organizations; (4) specific acquaintance with operational problems in college administration, including finance and planning, legal issues, student personnel administration, development, public relations, professional schools, institutional research, state coordination and government relations, research administration, administration of auxiliary services, personnel practices, faculty recruitment, libraries, property, community relations, and so forth; (5) knowledge of and ability to use the skills of disciplined inquiry in the social sciences. Recommended topics include description, inference, measurement, hypothesis testing and experimental design, alternative methodologies, bibliographic tools, and elementary computer programming; (6) comprehensive knowledge of the history of higher education, of college and university curriculum, of students' characteristics, of student development, and of student culture; (7) familiarity with learning theory, educational philosophies, with the forms and functions of education in other cultures, with varying theories of human behavior. The Teaching Option specifies the following: (1) a primary commitment to facilitating learning in students rather than the generation of new disciplinary knowledge through research; (2) skills to work with a student body of widely diverse interests, goals, occupational and academic background. Many of the students will have a distinctly non-academic orientation and interests toward practical vocational pursuits. Others will aspire to academic careers, but lack the skills to begin effective work in that direction; (3) a teaching specialty broader-based than that for upper-level or graduate instruction at four-year institutions of higher education. The knowledge and skills needed, for example, to teach psychology for college parallel programs may be very different from the knowledge and skills needed to teach psychology in the technical and occupational programs within the community college. Yet one faculty member is often called upon to teach in both programs; (4) a recognition of the guidelines for academic preparation and criteria for faculty rank as recommended by the Virginia Department of Community Colleges; (5) a recognition of the realities of the job market today for potential community college teachers. It is advantageous for the potential teacher to offer a second, related teaching specialty or to offer skills and knowledge useful in developmental programs for the academically disadvantaged students.

The curricular requirements in each flow out of these specifications. The administrative option includes, in item 5, research skills, but no special emphasis on doing research. The teacher option rather surprisingly ignores research although parts 1, 2, and 3 surely suggest that awareness and use of research would be useful to the teacher. No separate research option is described, and by this omission the Virginia program may be fairly described as practitioner–oriented. In view of the lack of clarity or direct attention to learning objectives in so many programs, this specificity in purposes and objectives is refreshing. Similar statements for the DAGS flow out of additional assumptions as the purpose of this diploma.

Another objective of most higher education programs, which can be lost too readily in the review of objectives focusing on majors in the field, is to offer courses which may be elected by graduate students in other fields or may be developed as a minor. In a number of universities, the prestige and the interconnections with administration have encouraged the use of minors by Ph.D. candidates in other colleges and departments. This relationship seems to have been especially developed in the health sciences where the rapid growth of new programs has made demands for academic-oriented health science teachers and administrators.

Organization of Programs

The unit in which the higher education degree program is based is designated in several ways: program, division, section, department, area, center, institute, and so forth. In some cases, parallel units exist on the same campus—one for research, another for instruction. Consultation and service may be provided by either or by both. Pennsylvania State University, for example, has both a center and a department. So have the University of Toledo, New York University, University of Washington, and the University of California, Berkeley. None of these units directly offers courses or degrees, although part or all of the center-associated faculty may be involved in graduate work and instruction through other units. Centers at the University of Virginia, University of Michigan, University of Oklahoma, and the University of Massachusetts appear from the literature to be primarily instructional units responsible for the degree programs. Institutes of higher education at the University of Florida and the University of Georgia apparently are responsible for instruction, research, and service. The terms institute and center are obviously used in universities with very different meanings. Table 1 indicates the roles of the institutes and centers at 20

Table 1.

HIGHER EDUCATION CENTERS AND INSTITUTES

Arizona State University	Center for the Study of Higher Education (mainly an instructional unit)
University of California (Berkeley)	Center for Research and Development in Higher Education
University of Colorado	Higher Education Center (mainly an instructional unit)
Columbia University Teachers College	Institute of Higher Education (future uncertain)
University of Florida	Institute of Higher Education (Service, instruction, research)
University of Georgia	Institute of Higher Education (Research, service, instruction)

Hofstra University	Center for the Study of Higher Education (mainly institutional research)
University of Massachusetts	Higher Education Center (One of several centers which are basic units in college of education)
University of Michigan	Center for the Study of Higher Education (mainly an instructional unit)
University of Minnesota	Higher Education Center (new designation, exact role uncertain)
New York University	Center for Higher Education Research
Oklahoma State University	Center for Educational Administration
University of Oklahoma	Center for Studies in Higher Education (instruction and research)
Pennsylvania State University	Center for the Study of Higher Education (research)
University of Pittsburgh	Institute of Higher Education (part of the Department of Higher Education)
Temple University	Institute for Higher Education (future uncertain)
Texas Tech University	Junior College Center (instruction and service)
University of Toledo	Center for the Study of Higher Education (research and service)
University of Virginia	Center for Higher Education (mainly instructional)
University of Washington	Center for Development of Community College Education (degree programs and services)

universities. When the institute or center is an instructional unit, we have assumed that research and service are inevitable accompaniments and have not checked these functions unless some special efforts are mentioned. Likewise, research units will usually engage in some public service. Institutional research may be done incidentally by all centers or institutes, but it appears as an avowed purpose in only three cases.

The distinctions among departments, divisions, programs, and areas are also idiosyncratic. Those listed here suggest only the frequency of the terminology and do not indicate any necessary similarity in structure or organization. We assumed that a higher education program included within a department or other unit not including higher education in its title was a program unless specifically indicated as a section, area, or division. Thus the figures showed 27 programs, 6 divisions, 2 areas, and 1 section. There were 11 separate departments (only higher education in the title), 10 composite departments (those that included higher education with adult, continuing, or some other specific indicator), 8 centers, and 2 institutes.

We did not attempt to resolve the niceties of these various designations, but we can provide from discussions, prior research on institutes and centers, and the literature the reasons for the varied nomenclature. For example, in some universities, centers, or institutes are research or service units. They may not offer courses or degrees. Tenure for faculty may not be possible except through departments and colleges. (Hence ten institutes or centers do not appear in the breakdown above.) Centers or institutes may be interdepartmental, intercollege, or even universitywide, thereby affording increased opportunity for affiliation of faculty members other than education. Because of their less formal existence outside the traditional university, college, departmental hierarchy, centers, or institutes may be created at various levels and organized in more informal ways. Some centers and institutes exist within departments, others within colleges, paralleling departments, and still others are all-university reporting directly to central administration. Such units may be formally or informally recognized by administrators rather than formally set up by governing board action. Institutes and centers with special designation and purposes have had, in the past, greater success in acquiring funds from government and foundations than traditional units. Centers and institutes provide, especially for the director, a title, unusual autonomy which can be used to attract or hold persons of outstanding stature who would neither be attracted by or satisfied within the departmental structure. The departmental structure based on disciplines is not altogether suitable to colleges of education (or other professional schools). In education, categorization by levels (elementary, secondary, higher), by disciplines (psychology, philosophy, sociology), by function (counseling, evaluation, administration), and by client (adult education, disadvantaged, women) make it difficult to find any organization which accommodates students' desires, faculty aspirations for unique status designations, and the external market realities. Thus higher education may be associated with several specialties, administration, student personnel, or split into adult, higher, community college. The college of education at the University of Massachusetts is organized around 13 centers and four noncenter programs: Aesthetics in Education, Foundations for Education, Foundations for Higher Education, Study of Human Potential, Human Relations, Humanistic Education, International Education, Study of Educational Innovation for Leadership in Education Administration, Educational Research, Media, Teacher Education, Urban Education, Reading. Other colleges of education use various combinations of department, division, program, and so forth.

The desire of those involved in higher education for an identity (in title and in unit designation) sanctified in published materials, local strictures on titles and designations, jealousies of other faculty members, the ambiguity of the designation *higher education,* and individual idiosyncracies, we believe, account for the range of designations noted. We do not detect much either in the way of an established rationale or in definitions which justify interinstitutional generalizations about the significance of these designations. Internally, however, they may have considerable significance in relation to autonomy in degree requirements, specificity of titles given to faculty, homogeneity in faculty, and a specifically designated budget.

Admission Requirements

Although concern was frequently expressed in regard to admissions requirements, we doubt that much of significance can be said about these requirements because programs vary so widely in their purposes and clientele. For example, a program which caters to experienced faculty members and administrators reasonably gives less attention to test scores than to career success and motivation for an advanced degree.

Admission requirements are not spelled out in detail in all cases and a committee review of the application, supplemented perhaps by an interview, appears to be more critical than any particular item. Most programs specify a master's degree and frequently prefers a degree in an academic field. The Graduate Record Examination Aptitude Test is recommended or required in many cases, with a minimum score of 1000 specified by several institutions. Alternatives of 900 on GRE and 1300 on the National Teachers Examination or at or above the 50th percentile on the Miller Analogies Test were mentioned in two programs. One program specified only an "acceptable" score on the GRE.

Other requirements include a four- or five-year degree, superior scholarship, a personal interview, prior experience in higher or secondary education or in related types of endeavor, and a personal information sheet, as well as the formal application. Letters of recommendation are often required. A written statement of purpose is specified for one program and another requires a statement of the expected major field of specialization and reasons for it. The University of California at Berkeley alone requires the Strong Vocational Interest Test.

Admissions requirements naturally vary with the degree sought—master's, educational specialist, or doctorate. When the doctorate is viewed in sequence with one or both of these lower-level degrees, admission to the doctoral program may well be predicated more on the quality of the prior work than on any other factor. Thus the master's degree is used in some programs primarily to screen out students unqualified to proceed to the doctorate.

The college of education admission requirements may be operative for the higher education program but are not always entirely suited to it. Yet our impression is that admissions are in the main made flexibly and perhaps somewhat uncritically for individuals of prior experience. We suspect that the practical outlook of many of these individuals and their dislike for statistics, research methodology, and theory courses give rise to the repeated expressions of concern about admissions. Nevertheless, our own predilection is that flexibility in the admission of individuals to a practitioner-oriented program is better than rigid adherence to test scores or previous grade-point averages.

Degrees

On the degrees offered, we acquired the following information: 17 offer the Ph.D. only; 15 offer the Ed.D. only, and 36 offer both. The distinctions between the Ph.D. and Ed.D. are not entirely clear. Some programs are restricted to the Ed.D. as the only doctorate offered in education; others use the Ed.D. for candidates oriented to educational leadership, administration, or educational practice other than research. In substance, based on review of requirements, the basic distinction between the Ph.D. and Ed.D. is whether their orientation is research or practitioner. However, the Ed.D. of one institution could be a Ph.D. at another, and the distinction has little to do with institutional or program reputation. In 17 programs, only the Ph.D. is granted, whether for a research or a practitioner orientation. In the 36 programs in which both degrees are available, the distinction between the two involves one or more of the following: foreign language(s) (or an approved substitute) required for the Ph.D., not for the Ed.D.; a more extended residency requirement for the Ph.D.; differences in the credits required in education and in a minor(s) or cognate(s) outside of education; field experience or internship for the Ed.D. but not for the Ph.D.; an applied or practical-problem approach to the dissertation requirement for the Ed.D. In some universities in which the foreign language requirement has been discarded or made optional for the college, department, or committee, the distinction between the Ed.D. and the Ph.D. has disappeared and the latter has become the preferred (or the only) degree. In the 14 programs where only the Ed.D. is available, the usual tradition or policy is that all education degrees are practitioner-oriented and that the Ph.D. may be granted only for basic research in a substantive discipline. Several programs reported the hope or expectation that this restriction might be lifted. Others apparently have found that the Ed.D. has achieved widespread acceptance in their area, and see no need to consider a change or student option. Of the 67 programs, 23 provide a doctorate, a two-year specialist or certificate program and a master's degree; seven offer both a doctorate and a two-year program; 18 include a master's degree with the doctorate; and 18 provide the doctorate only. (One was unclear.)

In 38 programs, a master's degree in higher education or in a specialty classified under that field is available. The one-year master's is predominant, but a two-year advanced master's degree is reported by two universities and a two-year master's in college teaching was reported by one. The master's degree is deemed useful for those needing to work before continuing with the doctorate, for community college teaching or administration, or as an adequate terminal degree for work in admissions, residence halls, placement, and so forth.

Two-year programs variously designated as Advanced Certificate, Educational Specialist, and Certificate of Advanced Study were reported. Adding to these the two advanced master's degrees, a total of 29 two-year programs (degrees or certificates) in higher education were reported by the 62 institutions.

The occasionally used Diploma for Advanced Graduate Study, familiarly designated as DAGS, was not reported in use.

The exact designation of the degree was requested in an attempt to learn just how the qualifier *higher education* is appended. Our request called for the officially approved designation as recorded on the transcript and diploma. The response was not altogether clear in some cases, and some do not formally designate the degree beyond education or educational administration. The 54 responses indicate different practices, and they break down as follows: In higher education there were eight Ph.D.s, thirty-two Ed.-D.s, two Ed.S.s on certificates, fourteen M. Ed.s or M.A.s. In education there were twenty-six Ph.D.s, seven Ed.D.s, six Ed.S.s on certificates, eighteen M.Ed.s or M.A.s. In higher education administration there were two Ph.D.s, two Ed.D.s, and three M.Ed.s or M.A.s (no Ed.S.s on certificate). We assume that the preference for *higher education* with the Ed.D. arises from the fact that this degree already incorporates education in its designation, whereas the Ph.D. almost always requires a general field designation. The use of the Ed.D. in a few universities as a teaching degree in a number of disciplines has perhaps contributed to the use of a parenthetical designation.

A few idiosyncratic degree designations add to the range of possibilities. These include: Ph.D. and Ed.D. in College Teaching; M.A. in Community College Teaching; Ed.D. in Junior-Community College Education; M.A. in College Teaching; Master's in Student Personnel Administration; M.A. (Education Administration-Higher Education). The variety in degree designation is of no great significance, although one might wish for more consistency. It is perhaps of more significance that of 39 responses to the question of the desirability of a master's degree in higher education—the no's (25) were more than double the yes's (12). Several respondents suggested that the master's might be discarded; several reported that it was used only as an out for those not able to complete the doctorate.

The two-year certificate or specialist programs may fill a need for community college personnel educated beyond the master's level but not requiring the doctorate. These degrees or certificates were originally regarded as terminal and offset from the doctorate, but literature received in this survey, as well as some previously collected, suggests an increasing tendency to view the two-year programs as intermediary between the master's and doctorate. Though we were told that candidates were cautioned that a master's or specialist program, whether terminal or a temporary stage toward a doctorate, may cause some loss of time, many programs offer these degrees in a sequential pattern.

Emphases or Specialties

Although one of the recurring criticisms of higher education both at the graduate and undergraduate levels is that it has been excessively fragmented, the number of specialties not surprisingly continue to show. Both students and faculty seek some unique identification which enhances their stature and employability, provides some sense of focus and unity, or permits a rational selection from an overly diverse array of courses, seminars, problems, and experiences. Such specialization is surely not intrinsically bad, but can become both confusing and costly because of curricular proliferation. Higher education programs are not immune to these tendencies.

The vast number of variables which may enter into characterization of specialties fall under the following categories: institutional complexity, level or type; institutional size; functions; source of support; sex; campus; individuals and groups (problems, needs and roles); echelons within institutions (organization, functions, problems, and governance); geographical and political (planning, coordination, systems, roles); disciplinary; service, problem, or clientele orientation.

According to institutional complexity, level, or type, they could be any of the following: technical institutes, community colleges, four-year colleges, professional schools, graduate schools, universities, urban institutions. By institutional size, they could be small, medium, or large. By function they could emphasize administration (finance, academic, personnel, facilities), instruction and curriculum, student services, educational services, research (pure and applied), public relations, educational media, teacher education. By source of support they could be private, church-related; private, church-supported; independent, public, or proprietary. By sex they could be for men, women or coed. By campus they could be residential, commuter, no-campus (external degree program), multi-campus, or branch campus.

According to individuals and groups they could be administration, faculty, students, business office, clerical and service personnel; governing and coordinating boards, state officials, general public, minorities, women, or adults. By echelons within institutions they could be departments, institutes and centers, schools, colleges, middle management, or total institution. By geographical and political category they could be institutional, community, state, regional, national, or international. By disciplinary classification they could be economics, sociology, psychology, history, anthropology, philosophy, communications, general education, or liberal education. By service, problem, or clientele orientation they could be land-grant, sea-grant, urban universities, state colleges, or state universities.

The preceding list includes only descriptive words or phrases actually used in course titles or descriptions. Obviously, the possibilities of developing courses and specialties by appropriate combinations of descriptions from these several categories is extremely large. A sampling of actual course titles follows. Although the terms and categories do appear repeatedly in course titles and descriptions, a direct examination and categorization yields a somewhat different pattern. Both the range and the specificity are impressive. Many of the categories are sufficiently represented in course offerings that each category may be regarded by a student as a field of specialization whether or not it is formally designated as such.

Foundation Courses: Overview of Higher Education, Current Problems in Higher Education, Higher Education and the Arts, Anthropology and Higher Education, Ecology of Higher Education, History of Higher Education, Sociology of Higher Education, Economics of Higher Education, Philosophy of Higher Education, Politics of Higher Education, Higher Education and Contemporary Society, University and the Community.

Levels and Types of Higher Education: Community College, Adult Education, Post-Secondary Occupational Education, Education for the Professions.

International Education: Higher Education and World Affairs, International Higher Education, and Comparative Higher Education.

Students: Student, Campus, and Society, The American College Student, Student Personnel Work, The Learning Environment, Learning Psychology for Adults, Interpersonal Relations, Recruitment and Admissions, Higher Education of Black Students, Student Participation in Governance, Campus Activism, and Student Personnel Work for the Culturally Different.

Curriculum: Curriculum in Higher Education, Curriculum in Vocational, Technical, and Health Occupations, Technology and Industrial Education, Curriculum Planning and Administration, and Curriculum Innovation.

Administration and Management: Organization and Administration, Administrative Decision Making, Administration of Student Personnel Work, Educational Leadership, Faculty and Staff Administration, Effecting Change in Higher Education, State and Regional Control and Coordination, National Systems of Higher Education, Higher Education and the Federal Government, The

Financing of Higher Education, Budgeting and Accounting Systems, Systems Management, Resource Allocation in Higher Education, Computer Applications in Higher Education, Financial Administration, Planning in Higher Education, Politics and Governance, Institutional Vitality, Legal Aspects of Higher Education, and Development Programs.

Teaching: College Teaching, Educational Technology, Testing and Evaluation, Academic Advising, and Psychology of Learning.

Research and Evaluation: Evaluation in Higher Education, Institutional Research, College Self-Study, and Research in Higher Education.

One especially interesting group of courses, mainly under foundation courses, couples basic disciplines or fields of study with higher education. Most of these titles (for example, Economics of Higher Education) are for a single course providing an overview which could be the starting point of a specialization.

Actually, the composite of the replies received to our question on emphases or specialties authorized for students seeking degrees in higher education identified 28 specialties. This number is arbitrary and could be materially altered by reinterpretation or alternative grouping. Should a specialty in general education administration be regarded distinctive or a minor variant of academic administration? The first could be either more general or narrower than the second. Since it was listed in one program as a specialty, we counted it separately.

In some institutions offering programs in higher education, adult education, student personnel work, evaluation, and educational technology were included as subspecialties within the broad field. In others, these were grouped with other educational programs or occasionally listed as separate fields but parallel to higher education. Some specialties seem to us to be unduly restricted: minority affairs, curriculum, curriculum and change, philosophy and middle management. Moreover, it is not always possible to determine what experience justifies designation as a specialty or concentration. Two or three courses, some individual readings, and perhaps a possible dissertation focus likely would be enough in most cases.

We found several institutions in which teacher preparation

for elementary and secondary education were included in the higher education program. These programs serve the needs of those seeking a position, either in colleges of education or in departments, which involve responsibility for special methods courses and possibly direction or supervision of student teaching. Such specialties in many universities are labeled Art Education, Business Education, English Education, Mathematics Education, Music Education, Physical Education, Science Education, Social Studies Education, Agricultural Education, and Home Economics Education. In most universities, these specialty degrees are designated as Ed.D.'s or occasionally as Ph.D.'s in discipline and Education. Since the ultimate emphasis is at the lower levels of education and the courses are normally quite different from those taken by students oriented to other specialties in higher education, the inclusion of the teacher-education specialty in higher education is of dubious merit.

We also found a number of programs with close ties to the health sciences. Emphases include prepraration for teaching and administration in academic programs in the health sciences at the master's, educational specialist, or doctoral level. A few provide special programs for those with terminal professional degrees such as the M.D.

University of Iowa includes among its purposes preparation of individuals for careers in health occupations education such as consultant, curriculum specialist, department chairman, head of health occupations education, head of hospital-wide in-service education. Preparation of physicians and basic scientists for careers in academic medicine is included and specific provision is made to grant 28 graduate semester hours toward an Ed.S. or M.D. or Ph.D. in basic sciences. This makes is possible for the M.D. or Ph.D. to complete an Ed.S. within one calendar year. The Ph.D. is also offered in Health Careers Education.

However, specialties recurring with reasonable frequency (based on 55 programs) are less than ten. They include academic administration (offered in 48 programs); student personnel administration (offered in 38 programs); community college administration (offered in 31 programs); financial administration (offered in 21 programs); institutional research (offered in 21 programs); research on higher education (offered in 20 programs), and planning in higher education (offered in 17 programs). Teaching (including college teaching, teaching of higher education, teaching in the community college, and a combination of instruction and curriculum) occurred as a specialty in 18 cases. In one form or another, curriculum appears eight times and the college student three times.

We caution that the numbers attached to these specialties are no more than rough indicators of the tendency to recognize special interests. For the purpose of a dissertation, most doctoral candidates will narrow their research focus, and this may or may not be regarded by the candidate and his committee as identifying a specialty. We were told that students and their advisers often identify a specialty by a dissertation topic and a few related courses even though it is not formally entered on the record.

There is surely some justification for distinguishing among academic, financial, and student personnel administration. Community colleges do have some characteristics and problems different from those of liberal arts colleges and universities. The specialty in research on higher education reflects a basic dilemma in higher decation programs. Presumably the Ph.D. is a research-oriented degree, but in many higher education programs it has become practitioner-oriented—geared to the preparation of administrators, teachers, or other personnel in a manner which other universities would insist is the function of an Ed.D. Institutional research involves a practitioner or applied research orientation and poses similar problems. Emphasis on planning in and of higher education is surely needed, but this emphasis, too, is practitioner-oriented. And the skills, concepts, and principles required in most of these higher education specialties are primarily drawn from other disciplines or areas of study. Perhaps higher education specialties, after all, represent distinctive foci only from looking ahead to special tasks and drawing upon appropriate disciplines and related experiences to provide professional insight and capability. Thus higher education is a specialty in its own right only to the extent that the individual views himself as a researcher in higher education (or some aspect of it) and as a teacher of courses labeled or characterized by a focus on higher education. But the individual who opts for such a career might develop it equally well by a doctorate in sociology, psychology, economics, or any one of a dozen other fields. Application of his discipline to the problems of higher education would also provide for teaching courses in higher education.

Some specialties are underrepresented when tabulated from a higher education orientation. Student personnel programs for higher education, adult or continuing education, and especially college counseling are perhaps as often offered independently as they are as a part of higher education. Even the community college program is occasionally viewed separate from higher education. On the other hand, several programs seem to be almost solely oriented to the community college; and one, the University of Toledo, states a major commitment to liberal arts education.

The conception of specialization in a program depends on the range of specialties. If adult education, community college education, and student personnel work are grouped with higher education, higher education may itself be viewed as a specialty.

The University of Southern California lists concentrations in adult education, the college student, community college, curriculum, fiscal affairs and governance, history and development, teaching, professional education, technical and industrial education, and the learning environment. In contrast, other programs list no specialties, although, as several respondents pointed out, students may identify for themselves a specialty by their own selection of courses, readings, internship, and research.

The University of Florida states that the higher education candidate can major in any one of five departments. Florida State University succinctly provides a justification for the specialty in administration by stating that the degree recipient should be "flexible enough to take on a wide range of administrative tasks and yet have sufficient specialization to claim an area of competency."

A document received from one of the universities already operating a widely recognized program in higher education indicates how a program may be expanded to serve additional purposes. Since the exact status of the proposal is still uncertain, and since our comments are in some ways critical (although with some empathy for the concerns voiced), the source and authorship of the document will not be identified. The program already prepares prospective faculty members for teacher education, higher education, professional scholars in the health fields, and administration in all levels of postsecondary education. The additional need is that of preparing individuals for administrative roles in the central office of a state system or in an individual campus administrative staff.

The argument presented for the expansion is that coordination and administration in a state or regional system has become so complicated that the tradition of selecting professors for administrative roles is no longer valid. A broader understanding of higher education is required and specific knowledge and skills are essential to managing a complex system. Undoubtedly this proposal partly arises from the recent reorganization of higher education in that state into a single system. The proposal also suggests that federal coordination on a national basis may be but a matter of time.

Accordingly, the proposal would add to a program already including courses on student personnel administration, curriculum, community college, higher education in the United States, teacher education in the United States, principles and practices of college teaching administration, and internship, a series of courses covering finance, program planning, budgeting; institutional research and management information systems; state coordination and control, consortia, federal agencies, nongovernmental agencies, and international agencies; higher education law and the courts; governance; curriculum development and evaluation; staff development and collective bargaining. The program would also include internship in campus offices and in the central office of the system. The proposal recognizes that staff expansion and close cooperation with the system and administration are necessary.

The concerns which give rise to the proposal are real. That the individuals needed to staff systems can or will readily absorb all relevant knowledge and skills for system coordination is doubtful. Yet we have some qualms about such a proposal; first, because the information collected from higher education programs suggests that numerous other programs have similar aspirations; second, because we doubt the approach through a multiplicity of courses will necessarily develop the insights and capabilities required for flexible coordination and continuing growth by coordinators; and third, because we doubt that a sufficient number of faculty members with necessary capability and experience are available to staff the courses and programs. Such an approach could result in training of bureaucrats seeking to move directly to the highest levels of administration without having assimilated the essence of the university and an adequate respect for the faculties, departments, and colleges upon which its success depends. We would be more inclined to explore the possibilities of inservice education of individuals who had already demonstrated some competency for administration and ability to maintain the rapport with and the confidence of the faculty, as well as of those persons and agencies external to the university whose continuing support is essential. In brief, we doubt that courses, even when accompanied by internships and research, can make an administrator, but boards, laymen, and legislators, we fear, might be influenced to think so, thus bringing about discord which may prevent the effective use of programs and resources.

Degree Requirements

Previous experience in attempting to summarize degree requirements indicates that reference to catalog (or other formal) specifications is risky. One reason is that catalog credit requirements are minimums; committees may and do require students to take additional courses because of perceived deficiencies or because the added courses are especially relevant to the individual's goals. Candidates sometimes propose excess credits simply because they want certain courses (or professors) on their record or perceive the courses as essential to their career. Many graduate advisers and committees consider the entire graduate program (master's, specialist, and doctorate) as the planning unit. This results in such marked variations in courses and credits in individual programs that the underlying principles and policies used in formulating a doctoral program are not apparent unless the total educational experience of each individual and the rationale for the planning of his program is consulted. Unfortunately this rationale is not usually available. The program reflects the agreements reached but not the reasons for them.

When programs are cumulatively planned, as we believe

they should be, even the undergraduate program may be relevant. An undergraduate major in business may develop significant competence in economics, accounting, or management to justify an atypical emphasis based on the undergraduate background and leading to an unusually strong specialty. An undergraduate major in mathematics, statistics, or computer science has similar potential. Many higher education professors prefer doctoral candidates with a master's degree in a field other than education. This emphasis, with or without additional supporting courses at the doctoral level, can provide a substantive teaching field. It can equally provide, as is the case with master's degrees in economics, accounting, management, mathematics, statistics, sociology, or psychology, a background for study of particular aspects of higher education, for institutional research, or for research on higher education generally.

We did not undertake to collect undergraduate and master's majors for higher education candidates, but were repeatedly told that most of them (other than perhaps student personnel work prospects) had taken much or most of their prior work in fields other than education. Again, this seems to us to be highly desirable. Because of these variations in background we found commendable the high degree of flexibility in many of the higher education programs. Individual planning with committee approval is surely more appropriate than rigid enforcement of specific course and credit requirements. But it is precisely at this point that attempts to characterize programs by catalog requirements fails, because cumulative planning, which admits that some requirements may have been met by earlier master's or undergraduate study, becomes almost as flexible as a program with no stated requirements.

Accordingly, we shall mention only a few variations in statements of requirements without necessarily assuming that specificity in requirements means rigidity in programming. The program at the University of Massachusetts (described as highly individualized and interdisciplinary in nature) lists very few requirements. The student must have one year of fulltime residence study. The comprehensive examination is developed by the candidate and the committee rather than being identical in part or whole for all students. No specific education requirements are stated. A dissertation or creative project is required. Both in course requirements and in the nature of the dissertation, these requirements offer almost maximum flexibility.

The University of Georgia requires 40 quarter hours in education, 20 quarter hours outside education, 5 quarter hours internship (three months minimum), 5 quarter hours dissertation (minimum), and a minimum of 85 quarter hours. Indiana University requires 90 semester hours beyond the baccalaureate spread as follows: major—45 hours including 15 for dissertation; first minor—12 hours minimum (can be in or outside education); second minor —15–20 hours (outside education). One basic course is required in each of these fields: research, educational psychology, educational philosophy, curriculum, educational measurement, and statistics. The University of Oregon requires 90 quarter hours beyond the master's degree and the following specific requirements: 9 hours in history, philosophy, or social foundations of education; 12 to 15 hours in research, statistics, and substantive conduct of research (these courses may be taken from educational psychology, anthropology, psychology, sociology and include practicum and internship); 30 hours interdisciplinary study; no language requirements or alternative; and 18 to 30 hours dissertation. The University of Denver requires a total of 90 quarter hours beyond the master's including 13 to 22 hours in education (not higher); 14 to 16 hours in higher education; 40 hours in a cognate; 20 hours in dissertation (which should relate cognate and higher education); and no internship. In addition, the candidate must meet a research tool requirement in a foreign language or 10 hours in research methodology.

These examples indicate the general nature and suggest the variables and range of requirements. The basic elements include requirements in total hours or credits, a residence requirement, and a dissertation. In more specific terms some combination of the following elements is usually required or recommended: core requirements in education, core requirements in higher education, requirements in research methodology, a specialty in higher education, practicum and/or internship, a minor within education, a minor or cognate outside of education, foreign language (or substitute), and dissertation. However, we found no program with formal requirements stated for each of these categories. Based solely on stated requirements the greatest variations appear in the existence and extent of *education* core requirement; *higher education* core requirement; internship requirements; research requirements, including dissertation; specialty requirement in higher education; and foreign language requirements.

The credits assigned to the dissertation may run as high as 35 to 40 out of 90 quarter hours, or as few as 5 to 10. Programs with lower dissertation credit presumably require more courses and seminars that may contribute directly to the dissertation. The foreign language requirement also affects the total course requirement. In programs with no foreign language requirement, obviously no substitute is required. When a foreign language is required, 12 to 15 quarter hours of other courses germane to the program often may be substituted by committee approval. Some programs specify that an alternative research skill must be developed. Thus, statistics, computer science, and tests and measurements or evaluation are common substitutions. Other programs accept as a substitute any bloc of courses approved by the committee, including education courses supporting the higher education emphasis. Accounting and the social or behavioral sciences are suggested in several programs.

Core Requirement in Education

Some programs in higher education are constrained by the college of education requirements, which specify common or core requirements for all doctorates. These requirements are usually limited to so-called foundation courses such as educational psychology, educational philosophy, educational sociology, and history of education. A requirement in research methodology or in statistics is occasionally included in this grouping. The foundations designation frequently appears in course titles; for example, Philosophical Foundations of Education.

Stanford defines a core by introducing categories of study: studies in curriculum and instruction; behavioral science studies; normative studies covering ideological, historical, and philosophical bases of higher education; and inquiry skills. This approach has the advantage of providing some justification for the core and admits more flexibility in meeting the requirements.

The core requirement in education—occasionally described

as *general education*—is not unanimously approved. One gets the impression in some discussions that the total education faculty believes the integrity of the doctorate in education would be endangered by elimination of this core for any group. In contrast, the higher education faculty and the students may view the general education as wasted effort, especially when the core courses virtually ignore the nature and problems of higher education. Foundation courses in a higher education core seem much more appropriate to professors and students whose entire experience and interest have been in higher education. The authorization of a distinctive degree, Ph.D. in Higher Education, seems in some cases to have been associated with a successful thrust for complete autonomy in setting the higher education degree requirements.

Higher Education Core Requirements

We attempted to determine whether core requirement credits in higher education might be related to the total number of courses offered. The number of courses offered in the various programs ranged from six or seven to well over twenty. But this count must be suspect because of the manner in which seminars are used. In some programs, a single seminar number may be used repeatedly to cover many different emphases, in others the numbering system may apply a separate number to each topic. In addition, the number of courses offered depends on the number of specialties subsumed under higher education. If community college education, adult education, and student personnel work are included, the number of courses is usually greater than when these fields are separately listed. It was evident that core requirements tended to expand either in number or in the alternatives permitted as the range of courses and available specialties increased. If college student personnel work is included in higher education, the higher education core may include a course on that field. In several programs, especially but not solely, when the number of available courses was limited, no core requirement was stated. Core requirements are not always stated in official documents, but may appear in informal mimeographed recommendations or simply be informal agreements based on staff discussions. Occasionally, core requirements simply include the introductory course or a sampling of the several specialties (or professors) included in a program. This suggests that core requirements are occasionally political compromises rather than scholarly decisions. They may play a role not unlike that of undergraduate general education requirements in distributing the credit hours and offering each specialty to attract the undecided student as well as provide an overview of the broad field of higher education.

Most higher education core requirements involve three to six courses with possibly some choice permitted, such as four out of an array of five courses, or one or two out of each of several groups of courses. A typical requirement may include Foundations (Nature, Issues) of Higher Education, Student Personnel Work, Community College, Administration. Courses in college teaching, curriculum, history are also frequent elements of the core. One of the more extensive core requirements included the following: American College and University, History and Current Issues, Research on the College Student, Academic Program, Organization and Administration, Research Seminar.

Internship

Program statements describing doctoral requirements leave a degree of uncertainty regarding internships. The University of Washington specifies an internship for its community college education program for administrators. The University of Georgia states that an internship is required—arranged by the internship coordinator with the president of an appropriate cooperating institution. The minimum of one quarter (fulltime for 12 weeks) may be extended to two or three quarters, depending on the individual's needs as appraised by his committee. Five to 15 credits are granted for the internship. Written reports are made at two-week intervals to the higher education internship coordinator. At least two on-site visits to the intern are made by the coordinator and a final evaluation report is prepared. In arranging internships, the cooperating institution is expected to provide room, board, and a satisfactory expense stipend. This support is essential for most interns, but the stipend is also regarded as desirable because it creates incentive for the intern and encourages the institution to make good use of the intern rather than to assign meaningless tasks.

Henderson defined a higher education administrative internship as a period of experience under direction of a college or university. The intern may be a degree candidate, a winner of a competition (postdoctoral fellow), or simply a person seeking experience and making his own arrangements.

The following principles are drawn in part from Henderson, but have been rewritten and considerably augmented. (1) Interns are supervised by a qualified administrator competent in counseling, as well as in administration. (2) Careful selection of internship requires consideration of the individual's prior experiences, resouces, needs, and aspirations. (3) A stipend, fellowship, or scholarship should usually be provided. (4) An internship (if part of degree program) is arranged by adviser, intern, and employer with specific agreements as to work, credit, salary, evaluation, time involvement, and period covered, as well as educational purposes to be served. (5) If possible, the experiences of the intern should be varied and progressive; exploitation through assignment of routine, repetitive work should be avoided. (6) Periodic reporting, evaluation, and consultation involving the intern and his sponsors both in the graduate program and in the host institution is essential. (7) Conjunction of internships with seminars encouraging background readings, internalization and analysis of experiences, and discussion of observations and problems with peers and advisers is desirable. (8) A complete record of internship experiences and an evaluation of them should be filed by the intern at the close of the experience. (9) An evaluation documented by specific observations should be reported by the supervising administrator to the student's adviser. (10) The adviser should provide his own added commentary and confer with the student on his success and his possible need for further internship. (11) University credit is sometimes given for internship experience and usually this is desirable. If done, the adviser or coordinator of internships should be responsible for certifying the credit and reporting a grade if required. (Pass/fail is frequently used.)

Since higher education specializations cover research and

service and teaching as well as administration, a discussion of internships must take some account of this broad conception. The range of experiences suggested as internships or their equivalent include: resident hall assistant, director of social activities, teaching assistant, teaching fellow, research assistant, counseling intern, aide, assistant, or sometimes assistant director to various student personnel administrators, directors, or coordinators, assistant or assistant director of externally financed research or service projects; and assistant in educational technology services, institutional research, evaluation services, dean or department chairman's office. This list can be almost indefinitely expanded depending on the degree of specificity. The assignments may be in the institution where the degre is sought or elsewhere. They may be formally arranged on a parttime or fulltime basis as a definite part of the individual's doctoral program. Experience prior to admission to the program, if carefully appraised, may be accepted in part or in toto to satisfy an internship requirement.

Degrees Awarded and Current Enrollments

To our query on degrees awarded and on the number of students currently enrolled, many of the responses indicated that exact counts were not available and even estimates were difficult. In some institutions no records of degree recipients prior to ten or fifteen years ago could be located. Furthermore, the definition of the degree varies so that numbers are not strictly comparable. The inclusion or exclusion of degrees oriented to community colleges, adult education, teacher education, college teaching, and student personnel can obviously make vast differences in either number of degrees awarded or candidates currently enrolled.

Institutional practices or requirements in defining active candidates also lead to difficulties in providing the count of candidates currently enrolled. Some respondents reported separately on fulltime and parttime students. Some programs counted all candidates still actively pursuing a degree whether currently enrolled or not. Some require all active candidates maintain an enrollment and pay a fee whether or not they are in residence or enrolled in courses. Others reported only students actually enrolled.

Recognizing these deficiencies, it still seems useful to provide some indication of institutions which have been especially productive of doctoral degrees (Ed.D. and Ph.D.) in higher education. The following listing results from our tabulation: Indiana University, 250 degrees; Michigan State University, 228; University of California, Los Angeles, 200+; University of Minnesota, 190 to 200; New York University, 172; Florida State University, 150; University of Florida, 150; University of Southern California, 130; University of Michigan, 129; University of California, Berkeley, 125; Ohio State University, 100; University of Pittsburgh, 90; and Columbia University Teachers College, 90 since 1964.

Other programs reporting 40 or more degrees granted in higher education include North Texas State University (85), George Peabody (60–70), University of Maryland (69), Washington State University (63), University of Denver (61), Pennsylvania State University (59), SUNY-Buffalo (52), Southern Illinois University (49), University of Chicago (45), American University (40), St. Louis University (40), and Stanford University (40). Although Oklahoma State University reported some 600 Ed.D.'s, the vast majority were awarded to individuals seeking the Ed.D. as a preparation for college teaching in a substantive discipline. Higher education degrees in the sense discussed here are apparently a relatively recent emphasis at OSU. Western Michigan University reported 60 degrees, but only a portion of the recipients are directly oriented to higher education.

The reports of current degree candidates yield the following approximate enrollments: University of Pittsburgh, 200; University of Florida, 170; New York University, 165; North Texas State University, 125 in administration and 650 in college teaching; Michigan State University, 125; George Washington University, 101; Indiana University, 100; Columbia University Teachers College, 100; University of Michigan, 90 to 100; University of California, Berkeley, 75 to 110; University of Denver, 80; SUNY-Buffalo, 78; Florida State University, 70; and University of California, Los Angeles, 70.

Other programs with 40 or more candidates include: Wayne State University (65), University of Washington (65), Boston College (65), Syracuse University (60), American University (60), Virginia Polytechnic Institute (58), University of Oklahoma (55), University of Massachusetts (53), University of Toledo (50), and Southern Illinois University (50), Pennsylvania State University (50), University of Colorado (46), University of Minnesota (45), and George Peabody (40). Again, Oklahoma State University presents a special case. Although reporting 180 candidates, approximately 150 are pursuing the Ed.D. in college teaching with emphasis on preparation for teaching a substantive discipline.

Nine universities (Indiana, University of California–Los Angeles, New York University, Michigan State University, Florida State University, University of Florida, University of California–Berkeley, Michigan, and University of Pittsburgh) appear among the first twelve both in degrees awarded and current candidates. Denver and SUNY-Buffalo have expanded their programs in recent years. The once extensive program at Ohio State has been quiescent for some years and its character and size for the future have been under reconsideration. It should be noted that the program at MSU developed rapidly in the late 1940s with the establishment of the Basic (later University) College. Many faculty members in that unit sought a degree in higher education much in the pattern of the current D.A. and the Oklahoma State University Ed.D.

For the many reasons already mentioned, we have some hesitation about indicating the total of higher education doctorates awarded to date or the number of candidates enrolled as of early 1973. However, totaling the various higher education degree recipients in our survey, we obtain 3409 inclusive of both Ed.D.'s and Ph.D.'s. Recognizing that some respondents were unable to account for degree recipients prior to the early 1960s and that some programs have been missed, 3500 to 3600 is not an unreasonable estimate of degrees granted to date in higher education. How much these persons really have in common in their educational experiences is an unanswerable question.

Current enrollment counts also present difficulties. Our total, based on the survey returns, is 4078. It is striking that reported current enrollments exceed by over 600 the total higher education doctorates awarded to date. We may well be on the verge of producing an oversupply, a fear expressed by some professors in interviews.

Positions Held by Degree Recipients

In many cases no information was (or could be) provided about the position held by doctoral degree recipients. In some only information on a segment of the graduates was available. In a few cases, essentially complete lists of graduates and initial or current position was provided. These institutions provide the basis for our summary of positions held. The institutions include: Michigan State University, 228 since 1956; Arizona State University, 32; University of Illinois, 15; University of Chicago, 34; New Mexico State University, 13; University of Arkansas, 30; University of California, Los Angeles, 157 since 1961; Boston College, 5; Florida State, 136 since 1958; George Washington University, 13; Indiana University, 242 since 1964; Southern Illinois University, 42; University of Washington, 35; University of Wisconsin, Madison, 11; University of Michigan, 107 since 1952; and University of Oklahoma, 21 since 1966.

Out of the 1057 higher education degree recipients for whom initial or current positions were available, about 77 percent were in four-year colleges and universities. Of the 77 percent, about 7 percent were listed under adult and continuing education. About 12 percent were in community colleges, about 1.5 percent in public schools. The remainder (about 6 percent) were employed in government, foundations, education associations, or business.

Thirty percent of the graduates were in teaching, counseling, or equivalent college positions. In all, 64 percent of the graduates are in administration and 15 percent have titles as presidents or vice-presidents. Another 31 percent hold deanships. About four percent (40) were reported as having become professors of higher education. The orientation of programs and students to administration is borne out by the 575 individuals reporting jobs as chairmen, directors, coordinators (122); registrars, librarians, business managers, institutional research (19); deans and public school administrators (278); presidential assistants (18); vice-presidents (59); and presidents or chancellors (79). Although adequate bases for comparative judgment do not exist, the record of administrative placements is surely satisfactory if that is the goal of programs and of students.

Although many degree recipients obtain administrative appointments as deans or presidential assistants immediately, only the unusually mature person is likely to attain a vice-presidency or presidency without several years of service following the receipt of the degree. Most higher education programs are only 10 to 15 years old or less and tended to be quite few in their earlier years, thus the success of these programs in preparing administrators is doubly underlined.

Faculty

Our survey, focusing on those with a doctoral degree program in higher education, cannot accurately identify all those faculty members who may be regarded, or who may regard themselves, as teaching or researching on some aspect of higher education. Based on listings from 62 universities our tabulation shows 213 fulltime faculty members and 321 parttime, for a total of 534. Mayhew previously estimated between 400 and 800, a safe range since at least another 10 to 20 universities offer courses if not degrees in higher education. Yet, even our minimal 534 estimate has in it elements of uncertainty. It includes some persons loosely affiliated with higher education who have never taught a course in higher education, never directed a doctoral candidate in higher education, and never executed a research study in the field. Usually these persons hold some administrative appointment and have a courtesy title reflecting their desire for some academic rank designation. As times even a president or vice-president likes to identify with the professoriate.

The count of professors of higher education is further complicated by the variations in designation and the informality attached to some of them. In some institutions all personnel in the college of education are designated as professors of education. Any further specification is parenthetical and unofficial. Some professors associated or affiliated with higher education hold titles elsewhere.

Thus the senior author is professor of university research, a university rather than a departmental or college designation, but spends a significant portion of his time in teaching, researching, and directing doctoral students in higher education. These irregularities—at least as viewed in reference to the practices in the traditional departments and disciplines—are not of great significance in one sense. But, in another, they reflect the unique nature of higher education as a field of study, instruction, and research. They certainly complicate or negate any accurate census taking. These loose affiliations obscure the identity and character of the field, but perhaps, on balance, the resources represented and the identification of administrators with higher education programs add strength and vitality rather than detract from the field.

The distribution of higher education faculty over the several ranks is of some interest. Of the fulltime faculty reported in our statistics, 55 percent were professors, 25 percent associate professors, 16 percent assistant professors, and the remainder (4 percent) either lecturers or instructors. We find some surprise at the reported titles of "instructor of higher education" on several counts. In recent years the use of the title instructor for anyone with the doctorate has disappeared in most institutions, and the assignment of either instructors or junior faculty without the doctorate to teach at the graduate level is, at the least, a dubious practice. In another sense, the stature of a field designated as higher education hardly seems to be buttressed by extensive use of assistant professors and instructors which, in our data, account for over 20 percent of the higher education faculty.

The parttime faculty, heavily loaded with administrative personnel, rather surprisingly shows an almost identical distribution over the ranks: 58 percent professors, 20 percent associate professors, 19 percent assistant professors, and 3 percent instructors or lecturers.

In view of our comment about the use of junior-ranking faculty in higher education programs, note that in 23 universities all the fulltime higher education faculty carried the ranks of professor or associate professor. To these should be added five universities in which higher education is staffed only by parttime faculty and all these persons are in the top two ranks. Thus, 22 of 55 programs are staffed by only professors and associate professors, although taken as a group, they are neither the largest nor the more prestigious programs.

The Department of Higher Education at one university lists thirty-one persons with academic titles in the department. The makeup of this group indicates one pattern of staffing which certainly adds luster to the department and creates acceptance and respectability in the rest of the university, but which (we suspect) tends to give a department a definitely practitioner tone. The large number of parttime persons could—we heard this complaint several times—pose problems in departmental operation and possibly throw an overload of advising and detail on the relatively small number of fulltime persons.

The staff includes four persons with administrative emeritus status (Chancellor, Vice-Chancellor, Provost), five central administration officers (Assistant Chancellor, Associate Vice-Chancellor and Associate Provost, Secretary of the University). Two deans (Education, Health-Related Professions), one Associate Dean (Education), one Assistant Dean (Arts and Sciences), two departmental chairmen, four directors and assistant directors, and one curriculum coordinator conclude the list of administrative titles. In addition, there are six professors (without administrative titles) all of whom have dual departmental affiliations, two associate professors, two lecturers, and one assistant professor with three affiliations. Three of these titles (chairman, higher education; director and assistant director, Institute for Higher Education) relate directly to the program.

The dually appointed faculty members provide interrelations with central administration, as well as connections with public administration, sociology, geography, psychology, Black Studies, behavioral sciences, dental medicine, and foundations of education. These interrelationships may generate the interdisciplinary or universitywide involvement which many higher education professors deem desirable, although the coupling of administrative duties with many of these connections must weaken their interdepartmental role in course and program development. The Health Sciences relationship found here is somewhat unusual, although not unique. Similar ties exist at the University of Kentucky, the University of Iowa, the University of Florida, and elsewhere.

Summary

Our survey demonstrates that higher education as a degree-granting program has reached significant dimensions in offerings, specialties provided, degrees available, in faculty, in degrees already awarded, and in current enrollments. Programs vary in definition and goals, and numerous issues and quandaries reported within programs become more evident throughout.

Some programs have clearly and explicitly delimited their purposes. Others have exhibited an expediency and an opportunism highly commendable in demonstrating a desire to meet identified needs, but only further diffuse programs already strained by attempts to accommodate preparation for researchers, teachers, counselors, student personnel administrators, academic and business administrators, and public service personnel in technical institutes, community colleges, liberal arts colleges, and universities. On one hand, the attempt to offer a wide range of courses highly specific to the needs of the heterogeneous clientele and, on the other, the failure thus far to involve faculty from the many other relevant departments places an almost unreasonable burden on the relatively small faculty associated with most higher education programs. Size relative to the task requires that this burden be examined in two senses: first, in regard to the teaching, research, and service load which falls on the faculty; and, second, in respect to the improbability that any small staff can encompass the range of talent and experience required to fulfill the mentorious task. It is not surprising that some faculty members voiced concern about the possibility of upholding standards in the face of this burden. One professor, who reported fifteen active current candidates, an indeterminate number in absentia working on dissertations, membership on fifty doctoral committees, a number of major committee responsibilities, several community and consultation projects related to his university role, stated quite candidly that he was unable to pursue any research of his own. Others echoed his concern. This does not augur well for the strength of higher education programs.

Case Example

The Department of Higher Education at Southern Illinois University at Carbondale can serve as a prototype of the programs in most large institutions. It is large (143 admissions since 1960), reasonably productive (forty-nine doctorates granted during that time), and dedicated to serving the region in which it is located. The faculty of twelve (seven full-time and five part-time) have a wide range of administrative and educational experience, which is respected by their students, who feel that the program fits them well for their future administrative posts. Although the primary purpose of the program is to prepare administrators, fifteen of its graduates have become professors, a phenomenon common to many graduate programs in education.

The academic part of the program is typical in that admission to the graduate school, the College of Education, and the Department of Higher Education is the first step in the process, followed by acquiring an advisory committee, gaining candidacy, taking courses (including thirty-six units of required courses), passing a preliminary examination, and completing a dissertation. Although the program attracts part-time students, all candidates must spend at least three consecutive terms in full-time study. The courses in higher education are also typical, dealing with administration and governance, current issues, student culture and development, curriculum and instruction, philosophy, finance, and junior colleges. The department also offers courses and seminars designed to develop competence in many different research techniques and strategies. Generally students seem quite satisfied with their courses and believe their professors to be extremely accessible, of high intellectual quality, and with profound influence over their professional development. However, students would like to see more research-oriented faculty and more intensive preparation in research methodology.

Such a description, however typical, does not reveal the strengths and the uniqueness of the Southern Illinois program. The higher educational community at Carbondale is a close knit group;

they obviously like to be together and to talk about higher educational problems. One ceremonial, for example, is to give each other or guests inscribed copies of recent books dealing with the field. Although the faculty is not highly oriented toward research, its members spend a great deal of time with their students or on their behalf organizing applied or internship activities and ensuring that they are adequately placed on graduation.

The department keeps track of graduates and reports on their activities through a periodic newsletter. In one issue, for example, placement activities are discussed, the birth of a son to a recent graduate announced, the plans of a newly created senate described, and the various off-campus activities of the faculty presented. In the same issue, the chairman of the department points out the continuing need to maintain a healthy awareness of the situation in the field, describes what Southern Illinois is doing along these lines, and ends his comments with a plea for information concerning likely positions for graduates.

The department chairman is generally regarded as a genius for his ability to locate funds for student support and job opportunities for those who pass through the program. Because so many of the faculty either have had or continue to have major administrative responsibilities at the university, students in the department are able to use the institution as an ongoing case study and seem to know the university better than many of the senior faculty in other schools and departments.

The program in higher education at Carbondale epitomizes the entire university. Southern Illinois grew from a regional normal school to a large multicampus university devoted not only to serving the needs of its region in orthodox ways but also to becoming a prime economic factor in regional development. The Southern Illinois region has been and still is an economically depressed area. Few industries have persisted and grown, and work opportunities have been limited. The university has created jobs, trained people to fill them, and created a network of direct social services such as speech and hearing clinics, all of which have placed the university in almost a feudal relationship to the society which supports it but in turn is nurtured by the institution. The program in higher education operates similarly. On one day its faculty may convince a consolidated school board to defer closing one of the three-year high schools which dot the region; on the next it may aid in converting the school to a community educational center which will then have job openings for recent graduates of the university.

In light of its purposes, the Carbondale program must be judged a strong one. It receives strong moral and financial support from the central administration; its faculty is dedicated; its students are hard-working, knowing where they want to go and seemingly getting there; and its curriculum has a logical rationale and a basis in reality. The lack of major faculty research and the paucity of theoretical considerations contribute to a less than vibrant intellectual tone to the entire program, but few programs in higher education do manifest a high degree of intellectuality. One hopes that ultimately some will. In the meantime, perhaps the best phrase to describe the program in higher education at Southern Illinois is "down to earth"—just as the region is.

Chapter Three

RESEARCH AND SCHOLARSHIP

*H*igher education degree programs generally have not produced significant research—nor are they likely to. The teaching load and the demands for advising graduates, plus other professional responsibilities, allow too little time. Some programs have selected professors for prior administrative experience rather than established scholarship; and heavily practitioner-oriented programs naturally tend toward practitioner-oriented dissertation research, which may be useful later either as methodological experience or as background for a professional role. But this seldom contributes significantly to higher education as a *field* of research. This is precisely why some programs award the Ed.D. rather than the Ph.D. to the majority of doctoral recipients.

Research Agencies

Research has been a major focus and product of the Berkeley Center for Research and Development in Higher Education under the successive leadership of T. R. McConnell, Lee Medsker, and Lyman Glenny. Center studies have been widely disseminated and read, yet their actual effect on American higher education is difficult to assess. Research at the Institute of Higher Education at Columbia University, under Earl J. McGrath, focused primarily on the relationships of liberal and vocational education and on the problems of the liberal arts colleges. The highly specific nature of the content and recommendations of some of these studies and the widespread concern and activity about them in colleges and in professional education probably resulted in more immediate impact. The centers at Pennsylvania State and the Institute at Georgia have produced numerous studies focused on local or state problems that have had broader relevance. Recently the Kerr Commission, subsidized by the Carnegie Corporation, has been more productive than any previous or current organization of a wide range of statements on almost every conceivable aspect of American higher education. These, too, have been widely disseminated, read, reported, and discussed. Just what will result from them is uncertain, for some knowledgeable observers including the authors of this book feel that the sheer volume, as well as the span of time, has detracted from their initial prestige and attention.

Many other individuals and organizations have engaged actively in research in higher education or supported it. Scholars in disciplines have sought to apply their expertise to the broad questions as well as curricular, instructional, and research problems in their own field. Regional agencies, such as the Southern Regional Education Board, Western Interstate Commission for Higher Education, the New England Board of Higher Education, the Education Commission of the States, and the regional accrediting associations, have sought through studies, reports, or policy statements to understand, affect, and improve aspects of higher education.

The U. S. Office of Education, the National Science Foundation, the National Endowment for the Humanities, and the National Institutes of Health, have supported studies and reports, as have foundations, especially Ford, Carnegie, and Danforth. Professional associations and societies, such as the American Council on Education, American Association for Higher Education, National Association of State Universities and Land-Grant Colleges, Association of Governing Boards of Universities and Colleges, American Association of University Professors, American Association of Junior and Community Colleges, American Educational Research Association, American College Personnel Association, National Vocational Guidance Association, Council of Graduate Schools in the United States, Association for Institutional Research, National Society for the Study of Education, American Association of Colleges for Teacher Education, and Association of American Colleges, by conferences, reports, policy statements, and studies, have directed attention to issues and recommended action on them. The recommendations and demands of disciplinary-based professional associations and societies and specialized accrediting groups often have major impact outside their specialized fields. But few of these demands are based on research and their validity as indicators of quality is dubious.

Studies and reports of the College Entrance Examination Board, Educational Testing Service, and the American College Testing Program, have affected admissions, testing and evaluation, advising and counseling, and financial aid policies. Studies by state coordinating and governing boards of institutional operations, policies, and roles often have the most immediate impact because of their relation to program approval and budgetary allocation.

Management studies and reports by the National Center for Higher Education Management Systems (NCHEMS) at WICHE have already received widespread attention. They may markedly affect internal data collecting and external institutional reporting, especially when the National Center for Educational Statistics of the U.S. Office of Education, and state program budgeting efforts require general usage of NCHEMS program categories and data definitions. Internally-oriented offices of institutional research are increasing, and many engage in studies which require data from comparable institutions and hence result in reports significant beyond the institution.

Lack of Impact

In thus briefly mentioning all these agencies, we have taken a very broad interpretation of research on higher education. Many, indeed most, of the reports and studies hardly meet the definition of research acceptable in the basic disciplines. They are not accumulative as is research in the natural sciences, and many studies are self-serving in that they seek to advance a particular cause—a discipline, a profession, a new field of study or research, or the interests of a group of institutions. Unfortunately, the more profound and far reaching the research and its recommendations, the less likely is any immediate effect. Thus many highly critical studies of graduate education, of undergraduate teaching, and of waste and curricular duplication have been largely ignored. Recommendations to eliminate or greatly modify programs, alter management practices, or change structure and governance patterns usually go unheeded. The reasons for this are easily found.

There are over 2400 institutions of higher education in the United States and over a half million faculty members. The private and the large state universities particularly are highly autonomous, with faculty members playing a major role in decision-making. These institutions differ in patterns of organization and in budgeting and data collection procedures. Their colleges and departments resist external intervention and ignore it unless the rejection causes them to lose funds or prestige. In the past, presidents and deans were often sufficiently powerful or influential to change administrative organization, programs, or curricular requirements with minimal attention to faculty concerns and essentially none to students. Today, administrators occasionally welcome (while denouncing publicly) external pressures which force changes they would otherwise be unable to bring about because of conservatism or recalcitrance of faculty and students. New money (federal, foundation grants, or sizable individual gifts), possible loss of funds (by withdrawal of private donors, state budget office, coordinating board, or legislative action), or loss of status or prestige (by loss of outstanding personnel or action of accrediting bodies) are currently the major means of effecting change. In time, collective bargaining may become another instrument of change not only in salaries, but in faculty load, curricular organization, and instructional staffing arrangements—as it has in public schools and in community colleges.

Opportunism, expediency, and competition have been more effective in bringing about changes in colleges and universities than has research. Indeed, institutional research and research on higher education have been influenced by and have contributed to this situation. Both the design and the interpretation of research depend upon values which, in themselves, often involve more opportunism and relativism than truths or facts to justify action.

Bases for Decisions

There are at least five bases for decisions in higher education: comparison, subjective opinions and judgments, theoretical or empirical models, absolute standards, and history or tradition. Comparisons may be internal or external. For example, an attempt to determine faculty load or to analyze the salary or tenure structure will require comparisons of loads or salaries in similar departments of the university, as well as at other universities. The desires of students, faculty members, or of external groups or supporters can lead to change in programs or in the addition of new ones. The demands of the scholars in a discipline or the recommendations of consultants may alter degree requirements or bring about change in class size or laboratory requirements.

The achievement of consensus frequently determines new policies, such as fringe benefits and promotion policies. The consensus may emerge from discussion, recommendations of study groups, or comparisons which are uncomplimentary to the local situation.

Theoretical or empirical models generally play a minor role in university decision-making, but a few examples can be found. The prevalent pattern of undergraduate distribution requirements is at least partly based on a theory and set of assumptions about the ingredients of a liberal education. Studies in some institutions have led to a recommendation that final grades in classes of reasonable size be distributed in some pattern such as A's, 5–15%; B's, 20–30%; C's, 40–60%; D's, 5–15%; and F's, 0–10%. This empirical approach is based on past practice and perhaps some assumptions (or theory) about the distribution of talent or motivation among students. Input-output, cost benefit, or cost effectiveness analysis imply an economic model used to assess the worth of college programs, but defining output benefits and effectiveness is difficult because of differences in human opinions and judgments.

Absolute standards are especially rare in this era. Student

grades, credits, and point averages are expected to be completely accurate and current, with anything less unsatisfactory. Attempts have been made to develop models under which almost all students, by carefully planned experiences and feedback, would completely master a carefully defined set of competencies. Some less direct attempts to attain absolutes have verged on the ridiculous. One university committee, trying to define a credit hour, ruled that "A student should receive one hour of credit for three hours of effort however expended." The rule was discarded quickly when its full implications were recognized later.

History and tradition play a major role in determining university policies and practices. There may be some justification for this, but history may be misinterpreted and mindless adherence to tradition is surely reprehensible. Foreign language and physical education requirements, as well as general education or distribution requirements, have been long and loudly defended in many colleges on grounds that a liberal education has always required them. Yet adequate and convincing evidence exists to the contrary.

Each of these approaches to decision-making has been used to achieve quality or excellence or to define and maintain high standards. But since quality and excellence are difficult to define, pragmatic values based on comparisons, subjective judgments, theoretical or empirical models, absolute standards, and history or tradition have influenced final decisions. Faculty, administration, friends, and alumni commonly seek to move an institution toward national stature and recognition. Hence institutions are in constant competition, seeking to enhance their support base by adding programs that attract particular groups or meet new needs. Thus, they operate often on the basis of expediency and opportunism, on feasibility rather than actual desirability. Numbers—size of student body, faculty, or budget and range of program offerings and specialties—are confused with quality. In a culture in which growth and size have long been accepted values, this is not surprising.

Contrasting or competing values have been used inconsistently to maintain or improve quality. Thus there is a continual push toward duplication and even of uniformity among institutions in programs, salaries of faculty, and even instructional patterns. Each attempts to imitate those higher in the imagined hierarchy of merit. Meanwhile uniqueness, actual or imagined, is valued and publicized, and used as a defense against any external inquiries. When institutions are called upon to justify high costs, they are usually attributed to uniqueness and high quality, though concrete evidence is never forthcoming. Demands for increased efficiency are often denounced as a threat to quality. Faculty propose changes in the name of increased effectiveness, but disagree on the objectives or the criteria for appraising them.

Equity, on one hand, and efficiency, on the other, are always somewhat at odds, balanced only by the expediency demanded by current pressures and need for support. Probably most institutional faculties would prefer a highly selected student body requiring minimum individual attention while assuring an output of able graduates acceptable in the best graduate and professional schools. Indeed, this would be the easiest and most efficient way to produce the educated manpower our society requires. Yet, in the face of demands for equity (equal opportunity) from the educationally disadvantaged, most institutions have modified their admission requirements to provide special programs and remedial courses. The availability of much-needed special funding for this purpose, has also influenced decisions. With their enrollments declining, some universities have suddenly found open admissions an attractive prospect.

This is admittedly a somewhat cynical, yet we think not unrealistic, picture of the procedures and values involved in decision-making in higher education. It is simply naive to assume that institutions will welcome research on their own activities and seek to apply the findings to their own improvement. Even institutional researchers probing into the vitals of their own institutions have learned that their studies are not always welcomed and may be both resented and ignored. Immediate impact is not to be expected unless the problem is crucial, with both an apparent need for decision and the certainty that a decision will be made. If research is to have an impact, a readiness for it must be cultivated. Some tact must be exhibited both in attaining this readiness and in presenting the results if institutional research is to be effective. An institutional researcher who fails to realize this and who becomes enamored of doing research for the sake of enhanced personal insight and increased stature among his fellows is not fulfilling his obligations.

The institutional researcher who does focus on institutional problems and aspires to affect institutional policies will find that the values of faculty and administrators often differ from those assumed or anticipated. One study of 200 students initially denied admission because of their records but admitted by administrative direction demonstrated that only five remained in college after two years. The finding seemed to the researchers to justify existing admissions criteria. But when the administrator commented, "Just as I thought, some of these individuals can succeed if given the chance," the focus immediately shifted from efficiency to equity. Clearly, research findings become definitive only when viewed in relation to goals and values.

Institutional Versus Pure Research

To what extent do these observations apply to research conducted in higher education programs and research centers? The answer is neither obvious nor simple. Institutional research is directed to problems and decisions within institutions or systems of institutions. Comparisons, opinions and consensus, models, standards, and tradition play a role in conduct, interpretation, and decisions emanating from institutional research, we have already suggested. But the final decisions may hinge on institutional aspirations or system concerns rather than on national concerns and needs and appropriate institutional roles, policies, and practices. Research on higher education, in contrast to institutional research, may be conducted for many reasons: individual curiosity, increased personal understanding, theory development or validation, basis for policy formulation, arousal of interest and concern, or influencing the opinions and the decisions of certain groups in the higher education enterprise. Whether research findings really influence decisions is not easily ascertained. Research in the social sciences seldom, if ever, justifies unambiguous recommendations. Hence recommendations must either represent researcher bias or be of an if-then nature—if these results are desired or if you believe this, then the following courses of action seem desirable. Even so, personality and bias may outweigh other considerations. For example, cost-benefit analysts disagree on whether the primary benefits of a college education accrue to the individual or to the society, on the procedures to be followed, and whether to include such items as income foregone. Perhaps even more basically, they differ on whether social benefits, or only economic ones, are significant. And ultimately the economist's view of social and individual benefits determines whether he believes that the individual or society should pay the larger proportion of costs. A few years ago prodigious numbers of studies of alienated and activist students were produced, with contradictory analyses and conclusions. Although these groups probably never exceeded 15 percent of the student population, their visibility and vocality made studies about them newsworthy out of all proportion to the studies' significance or to the possibility of constructive action.

Yet, as in other fields, we are inclined to believe that pure research on higher education should be encouraged, for it may lead to insights which research directed only to solving an immediate problem may not. While it may not produce immediate action, we are convinced that increased knowledge and understanding does ultimately benefit decision-making.

Research on regional and national issues is certainly less likely to affect institutions than that focused directly on their immediate problems. But broad research may have impact in other ways: (1) by influencing the views of individual leaders to bring about changes consonant with the findings; (2) by affecting the development of new institutions which, untrammeled by tradition, commitments, and faculty antagonism or lethargy, may incorporate new ideas and recommendations; (3) by influencing the views of politicians, government officials, foundation executives, prominent laymen, and citizen groups who may, in turn, influence appropriations, gifts, and higher education planning; (4) by influencing through courses on higher education students who will ultimately play significant roles in influencing decisions as faculty members, administrators, governmental officials, or coordinating board executives in state systems.

Role of Research

Accordingly, we are convinced that all candidates for degrees in higher education should have extensive exposure to research studies. Whether they become teachers of undergraduates, professors of higher education, or administrators, they should be aware of the available research literature and of individuals, centers, and offices which conduct research. They should become familiar with the journals and other publications in which research is reported. Even candidates for degrees in other fields who take higher education courses should learn that information continually accrues on any given topic. In brief, all courses in higher education should emphasize higher education as a growing body of knowledge and help the student become sensitive to the major issues, points of view, and the studies supporting these views; and to encourage him to formulate his own views and defend them by reference to research. He should be aware of problems not yet answered and of assumptions and value differences which may influence interpretations and decisions. In seminars, he should be confronted with problems arising in universities and asked how he, as a teacher or administrator, would proceed. He should also learn that some decisions supported by research may be impractical or impossible because of tradition, entrenched interests, or concern for the individual welfare or the maintenance of morale and rapport. Change, however logical and defensible on the basis of research, generally comes about in lasting manner when most of those involved are convinced that change is desirable. The success of any innovation in a university depends on the cooperation of those affected, and change can no longer be imposed and enforced by administrators. Even if the forms of change are adopted, indifference, resentment, and active antagonisms will destroy the spirit and, hence, the desired effects.

These comments may seem unnecessary and even naive. Yet we believe they are justified because courses in higher education can and have sometimes become experiences in amassing a body of facts—names, principles, theories, and conclusions—with limited awareness of continuing accretion and possible change in these facts and principles and essentially no understanding of how they are to be applied effectively in institutions dominated by disciplinary-oriented faculty members and by students, each convinced of the validity of his own views and suspicious of or antagonistic toward innovations which would disturb existing patterns with no obvious advantages to themselves. By this approach, we believe that a corps of professors and administrators could gradually be developed.

Members would be aware of higher education studies and of institutional research studies within their own institution. As they maintained continuing contacts with such research and found that it modified their own views, they could, in turn, convey to others their convictions and reasons for them and thereby become instrumental in molding the opinion of those who would ignore or doubt the validity of any research challenging their own views and threatening their present status and stability.

Since most higher education degree recipients are, as we have seen, likely to become practitioners (teachers or administrators), we believe that the previous comments aptly describe the importance of the research exposure for the majority of students. However, to understand research as something more than just a body of facts, each candidate must develop some sophistication in reading research, in appraising the adequacy of its techniques, and the generality of its results. For most prospective practitioners this means, at a minimum, a consumer-oriented exposure to statistical methods sufficient to provide understanding of basic methodologies, assumptions, and interpretations. And surely all potential administrators should have some grasp of budgeting and finance, since any significant change in institutions is likely to have financial implications.

For those who would themselves become researchers, the prescription is complicated by the range of problems and techniques. A student of the history of higher education may require little more than some descriptive statistics and a thorough understanding of historical methods. Specialists in economics and finance will need accounting, auditing, some statistics, and possibly econometrics. Those studying students, faculty, and the impact of teaching methods and curricula on learning should be skilled in statistical methodology, testing and evaluation, survey techniques, and computer science. Only a few higher education programs have the facilities and faculty to provide such depth; programs which aspire to train researchers must seek both to coopt faculty members from other disciplines and to involve their students in significant research elsewhere in the university or outside the university. Courses alone, however excellent, are not enough. And programs to develop researchers must be planned and carried out by a faculty heavily and continuously involved in research. As we have repeatedly noted, this seems not true of the majority. Despite the value of practitioner-oriented programs, the future reputation and impact of higher education as a field of study depends on a relatively small number of research programs. From them will come the research which may ultimately alter and improve higher education; and from them also will come the professors of higher education capable of providing the important though lesser research emphasis required in other programs. This does not negate the value of programs to prepare practitioners, but it does suggest that their success may continue to rest largely on faith, until research yields a sounder basis for training administrators and for directing decision-making processes.

Scholarly Components

Apart from what weight to give research training in programs of higher education, there ought also to be some agreement with respect to other components of the domain, to the techniques of analysis, and to the attributes of those in the field. A number of components properly could be the object of scholarly inquiry, reflecting what is actually being examined and written about and what is now being taught in courses concerned with higher education.

Topics

First is the topic of administration, organization, structure and government of higher education, whether in a subunit of a specific institution, a total institution, a system of institutions, or the various educational bureaucracies and agencies. Included would be studies of the characteristics of faculty senates, roles assigned to various administrative officers, systems of institutional control and relationships between faculties, administration, governing boards, students and other constituencies. All are comparatively well represented in the literature of higher education, although frequently at the anecdotal, descriptive, or survey levels of analysis. Presidents, deans, and a few administrative subspecialties such as directors of admissions or directors of institutional research are described. Boards of trustees and statewide systems of government, types of faculty organization, collective bargaining agents, and the organization of institutions, or the changes in their administrative and organizational structures are studied.

Economics, financing, and financial management of higher education also should be covered. Appropriate work has been or could be done concerning ways of deploying the nation's resources for higher education, analyzing the claims of other contenders, the technology of allocating them to various constituencies, and the techniques by which financial resources are actually converted into educational processes and then to educational products of economic value. Although critical, this cluster of concerns attracted relatively scant scholarly attention until the latter 1960s. Few standard textbooks on financing higher education dealt primarily with budget making, budget control, and accounting. Studies of the relationship between cost and subsequent economic status of college graduates have been rudimentary; nevertheless, periodically, broadly based arguments, largely normative in character, urge this, that, or the other change in social financing of a system of higher education. More refined cost-benefits studies and budgeting techniques to maximize achievement of educational goals have been made only recently.

The third matter central to an understanding of higher education is teaching and instruction. The largest part of an institution's budget goes for faculty salaries. Yet outside of polemical pleas for improved teaching and instruction and a few studies on the dynamics of college teaching, the subject is relatively untouched. The interest in teaching and instruction that began to flourish at the end of the 1960s (as reflected by increased uses of student evaluation) could encourage substantial research and scholarship on the subject. However, teaching and instruction may be viewed by faculty members so highly personal that their nature will essentially remain a mystery.

Related to the processes of teaching and instruction are the categories of counseling, testing, guidance. Testing has developed the most extensive research base; counseling and guidance have developed elaborate theoretical rationales. Why the latter have not produced similarly elaborate compendia of research studies seems odd, since preparation for student personnel work has been one of the two largest subconcentrations in programs of higher education. In contrast the research base in testing is and has been relatively deep. Yet, few, if any, programs in higher education systematically produce graduates professionally qualified to engage in systematic and sophisticated testing activities.

An almost new component of the field of higher education covers legal provisions, legal interpretations, and the implications for higher education of precedent and legislated and administrative law. As late as the mid-1950s only one generally available book dealt with the law and higher education and scholars in law schools were seldom concerned with higher educational issues. The courts refrained from intruding into higher educational matters and state legislation was fundamentally parsimonious. However, as constitutionalism became more significant within institutions, as states created elaborate educational superstructures, as the cost of higher education increased, and as campuses became scenes of disturbance, the law became more central. This tendency seems likely to continue, especially if collective bargaining becomes widespread. One can even envision programs to train people both in in-depth exposure to the law and to general study of higher education.

Another major, expensive component has received relatively little attention except for description and exhortation is the curriculum, including those of the professional and graduate schools. Much has been written in a pleading tone concerning the liberal arts and sciences. Systematic evaluation has been made of programs of general education and professional school faculty have analyzed their curricula and produced recommendations with broad applicability. However, more recent curricular developments such as *ad hoc* courses, interdisciplinary studies, and some graduate work in arts and sciences have not attracted attention among those studying higher education. Yet the field is fertile and the alternatives varied. Some argue that the curriculum is so inextricably woven into a single subject discipline that no one outside of physics, chemistry or geology is capable of dealing in a systematic way with research structure, with curricular structure, or the outcome of a curriculum. This parochial view, however, is denied by the generalists who contend that these and other questions can and must be examined across disciplinary or organizational lines. Thus the curriculum still has great potential significance in some future encyclopedic synthesis of higher education.

Yet another important but scarcely studied element is the matter of purposes, goals, and values of higher education. Virtually every institutional catalog, of course, describes institutional goals. State studies and state master plans delineate broad social goals of higher education. Faculty discussions about education almost invariably cover purposes and goals. Yet how purposes and goals are perceived by different constituencies have rarely been catalogued; their philosophic presuppositions have rarely been examined. How purposes and goals of institutions are consistent or inconsistent with other social developments or how they have or have not been achieved have not been adequately assessed. If the essence of higher education is philosophic, its purposes and goals and values should preoccupy scholars working in the total domain. This is not to say that there are not philosophic statements. Collections of presidents' speeches, conferences proceedings, extended essays are all somewhat philosophical, but relatively few people, except Henry David Aiken, have used the approaches of formal philosophy to study the purposes of higher education. If values and goals are as significant as contended, then at least a few future research workers should be stimulated to focus on them as a major interest.

Higher education is a people-using and a people-processing undertaking; the faculty, staff, and administrations who are used should be as much a focus of study as the students who are processed. Students have fared much better; significant work has been done on intellectual and attitudinal characteristics of students and their paths through the system. However, not nearly as much has been done concerning faculty. Once one has examined Logan Wilson's *Academic Man* (1942), Caplow and McGee, *The Academic Marketplace* (1958), and a few others, the literature is virtually silent about how faculty members enter the profession, what kinds of people they are, how they proceed in their careers, and how they succeed in their professional tasks. These two matters should loom especially large during the 1970s and 1980s, as institutions try to make better use of their faculty resources.

The economy of higher education involves some of the preceding concerns, but is in another sense discrete. Economy here means the relationships among all higher educational activities in a given region, such as—at a very crude level—that involving the private institutions, the public junior colleges, state universities, and the University of California. This topic presents some interesting theoretical and mythological questions and can be of enormous practical value as well. For example, the 1970s have seen a growing interest in institutional mergers and complex consortiums, yet no available studies can help an administrator predict the impact on enrollments if an institution with an established name merges with another, changes its name, and possibly changes its mission as well.

The examination of types and levels of postsecondary education has attracted considerable attention and is likely to attract even more. There have been several analytical treatments of graduate schools as well as descriptive and quasianalytical treatments of predominantly black institutions, technical institutes, Catholic colleges, and others. But a wide variety of other postsecondary educational activities is emerging and will require scholarly attention. Proprietary education appears to be increasing; correspondence education is becoming a larger enterprise as is adult education, not only in connection with junior colleges, but as parts of four-year institutions as well. The University Without Walls and the multicampus institution extending over a vast expanse include many different types of postsecondary education. Indeed, a well-developed taxonomy of types of institutions and quasiinstitutions could provide an agenda for several research institutes. Unfortunately, this kind of study requires travel and visitation, making it somewhat expensive for an individual. Hence, opportunities to develop theses in this area are somewhat limited. Studies of educational institutions using only questionnaires generally lack a sense of reality.

Of a completely different order and appealing to only a few persons but still an essential part of higher education is the study of buildings and facilities of higher education. Experiments sponsored by the Educational Facilities Laboratories have suggested that the study of space and space utilization can be intellectually demanding, producing not only broad generalizations but also principles and practices of considerable economic and educational value.

As the public sector of higher education increases and institutions of higher education impinge more and more directly on local, state, regional, and national communities, political relationships assume greater significance. Analyses of political relationships are in their infancy, but include a few studies of the impact of the federal government on institutional policies and a few attempts to examine the economic impact of institutions on a community. Here is a highly complex area, clearly susceptible to study without demanding more research technology than currently exists.

Various policy questions may need study or require other kinds of research. The literature of higher education itself is a suitable and appropriate focus for scholarly attention. Higher education has been notoriously ill-served bibliographically. Content analyses of existing literature could document the weaknesses of research in fields already discussed. Assimilating, synthesizing, and interpreting research literature so that it may be read and used could benefit the almost one million persons professionally involved in higher education.

Research Skills

Even more difficult than defining appropriate substantive parts of the field is the task of identifying tools of analysis and necessary disciplinary competencies. In one sense the principle techniques for analysis are relatively few and are applicable to the entire domain of higher education. A would-be scholar should possess enough knowledge to recognize the existence of an unsolved problem. He should be broadly acquainted with the literature so that he can view it in perspective, and should be able to analyze and reduce it to manageable proportions. Some problems require facility in mathematics, statistics, psychometrics, or computer science; otherwise, all that is necessary is critical or analytical thought allowing one to sense a problem, examine assumptions, test the validity of evidence, and reach tenable conclusions. Specific technical skills are relatively easy to acquire. The ability to construct questionnaires, inventories, attitude scales, or interview schedules can be developed with a little bit of didactic assistance followed by practice. No large amounts of time are needed to prepare a person for historical research; the differences between primary and secondary

sources and the evaluation of the validity of documents can be quickly developed. Whether one is making a sociological, historical, political-scientific, or philosophic study, the important ingredients are an in-depth awareness of a relevant literature and the ability to use it.

The fields or disciplines relevant to higher education as a field of study include history and biography, sociology, psychology and social psychology, anthropology, economics, political science, philosophy, law, and such process fields as systems analysis. The fields of mathematics, statistics, foreign language, and computer utilization, of course, are of a different order. The domain can be portrayed as a two-dimensional grid, with administration, organization, and governance, curriculum, purposes, goals, and values, or political relationships on one axis and disciplinary fields such as history, anthropology, or philosophy on the other. The problems of the field of higher education, can be displayed on this grid. These include academic degree-granting activities, proprietary schools, adult and continuing education, graduate and professional education, and even correspondence education as long as its focus is postsecondary, although operational limitations may narrow research activities to colleges, universities, junior colleges, and closely related institutions.

Who does and who should do research and scholarship in higher education? Research here is like that in virtually all other fields, with the exception of certain kinds of medical research: it requires neither credentials nor formal preparation. To obtain support for research increasingly calls for credentialing, but if the support can be generated, a journalist can do respectable historical research or a physician a sociological inquiry. Although those currently involved in research and scholarship in higher education display appropriate academic preparation and credentials, a high proportion use approaches different from those of their own academic preparation, underscoring the possibility that the amateur or primitive can engage in research and scholarship. Thus T. R. McConnell shifted from psychology to university administration to his studies of governance and of comparative higher education. Evan Sanford moved from psychoanalytically-oriented clinical psychology while G. Kerry Smith, who contributed so much to higher education, entered the executive secretaryship of the American Association for Higher Education out of secondary education via work in the U. S. Office of Education. As a group those who have received formal preparation through departments of higher education have not been particularly productive as scholars and research workers; relatively few of the books published by Jossey-Bass or by the Carnegie Commission on Higher Education have been written by persons holding a doctorate in higher education, nor are many of those reviewed each year by Mayhew the works of writers professionally prepared in higher education. Perhaps this is because departments of higher education are administratively lodged in schools of education with would-be administrators as primary clientele rather than faculty members and professional scholars and research workers. Should this situation persist, higher education is likely to remain disorganized and lack the prestige and visibility of professional fields such as engineering, medicine, agriculture, or theology, which prepare practitioners as well as those who undertake research and scholarship. It is a central belief of the authors that scholarly activity has developed and reached such magnitude as to require formal definition, codification and recognition if further growth is to occur.

Perhaps programs in higher education might copy medical education, which prepares medical students to move toward either research or practitioner careers, by providing the common intellectual base in the natural sciences upon which both rest. A four-year doctoral program in higher education might consist of four component parts, each consuming approximately one-fourth of the total. The first would include basic studies essential for either a practicing administrator or scholar—relevant materials from the social sciences plus those designed to develop a broad awareness of the nature, functioning, and complexity of American higher education. Next would come an intensive study in a relevant discipline focused on problems of higher education, and some additional work involving a more sophisticated view of the complexities of higher education. This period, which might be called contextual studies, could be organized according to the career aspirations of the student. A prospective scholar's year might be divided four-fifths in economics or an alternative social science and one-fifth on higher education; a prospective practitioner's might be interdisciplinary, focusing on economics, political science and sociology for four-fifths of the work, with one-fifth focused on the subject of higher education. The next fourth would be a field of concentration— either a reasonably rigorous dissertation or a year-long carefully supervised internship supplemented by a paper relating the actual field experience with relevant literature, evidence, and theory. The last fourth could be designated as liberalizing or broadening studies, largely elective, to allow students either to explore the other arts and sciences or to work in other professional fields. This component might be met by a prior master's degree, or for those holding only the baccalaureate, could be used for work outside the college of education.

This illustrative program differs markedly from most existing programs, both in total requirements and in those specific to higher education. The latter, including internship and dissertation, might encompass only 35 percent of the total requirements, while the overall requirements would exceed those specified in many programs. Even so, this program still would not equip a graduate to compete on equal terms with persons having a doctorate in one of the disciplinary fields. A Ph.D. in economics will have different attributes from a Ph.D. in higher education, even when the latter concentrates on economic research. He would probably not expect to contribute to fundamental economic theory but his year's exposure to economics should permit him to apply appropriate economic theory to certain phenomena of higher education. He would not qualify for tenure in an economics department but he would certainly be appropriately educated for a department of higher education.

This curricular structure still does not accommodate the needs for competency in statistics, mathematics, computer science, or languages, all of which seem likely to become increasingly important. Despite the four year program there simply is not enough time. One solution might be more rigorous admissions standards, requiring one of these competencies or calling for additional study if a candidate were deficient. This requirement would then be an addition to basic requirements, as the foreign language requirement formerly was. Applicants might be required to have had mathematics through the calculus and to devote additional time to statistics and computer science if needed. Such standards might prove burdensome for many students but are not unreasonable if the goal is to produce more competent research scholars. Indeed, the requirements compare favorably with those in other scholarly fields; candidates in anthropology or history simply accept that a command of languages is essential. Research in higher education is not likely to be impressive unless researchers are well trained. Some of the practitioner-oriented programs must give more attention to understanding research if administrators are to understand and use it.

Purposes Served

Thus far this emerging profile has been examined from the standpoint of suitable subjects for study and appropriate techniques for analysis. Additional insights can be supplied by examining the purposes served by scholarly work in the field, purposes served by training programs, and criteria which justify support for formal programs in higher education. Scholarly study and research concerning higher education seems to be undertaken to achieve any or a combination of several purposes. First, there is simply the matter of scholarly curiosity. Some scholars would like to understand how and why statewide systems of coordination and control have developed simply because they represent an unexplained phenomenon. Curiosity certainly plays an important role but one suspects that possible applications to practice are considerably more significant. Research is to establish relationships and to determine principles upon which practice can be based. Recent efforts to apply organizational theory to higher education reflects this search, which is not primarily to reify theory, but to test principles and to learn if they can help an administrator. Research undertaken to permit evaluation and judgment is also practical. During the late 1960s and early 1970s considerable attempt was made to understand how complex systems of institutions functioned. A major motivating force was to provide advice whether existing structures should be modified or major changes made. Much research dealing with the impact of college on students is of this evaluative nature, designed to answer ultimately such questions as how to maximize impact to justify cost. Research also attempts to provide a basis for policy recommendations and policy-making. Much of the work sponsored by the Carnegie Commission on Higher

Education is clearly of this type, beginning with an examination of various models for federal support and ending with the alternatives by which institutions could relate more intimately to their urban surroundings. Of equal significance is research designed to help interpret higher education to the various concerned publics. During the late 1960s, antagonism toward higher education soared along with costs and campus unrest. The public began to demand accountability, spawning considerable research to help higher education explain itself in an accountable fashion. And obviously much research is intended to help practice. Studies of the relative effectiveness of different teaching techniques presumably assist faculty members to make choices among teaching styles. Studies of faculty governance structures are designed to help institutions adopt the most effective structure, while studies of the presidency are designed to aid presidents perform better in their difficult role. Finally, research and scholarship is designed to establish and test theories concerning the operation. This particular purpose has not figured largely among active scholars but a cogent argument is that if higher education is to emerge as a respected and viable domain of research, greater attention must be given to theoretical considerations.

The nature of the field of higher education must also be related to its educational programs. Departments, institutes, programs, and centers cannot avoid an educational or training function, with much faculty activity determined by educational purposes. First, and undoubtedly the most prevalent of the longstanding programs in higher education, is the preparation of generalist administrators. It is assumed that people who are given some notion of administration and organization and some understanding of the nature of higher education will probably make more effective administrators than if they acquire those insights the hard way. Increasingly, there has been a demand for people prepared as specialists—particularly, at first, as student personnel workers and junior college administrators but even these programs remain quite general; in fact, many appear to differ little from those for general administration. But several technical specialties have emerged, such as those for directors of institutional research, directors of space planning, and financial officers. Only a few of the larger programs have created curricular subspecialties, but the increasing demand suggests that programmatically this may be one of the next phases of development. A third purpose of educational programs is to prepare individuals to be college teachers through courses on the nature of higher education and some training in appropriate skills of college educational pedagogy. A few programs, such as that at Oklahoma State University, make this their primary purpose, and in a few institutions this task actually predated the creation of a department or center for higher education. A few programs have provided a general or liberal education service to undergraduates. The State University of New York at Buffalo developed several courses to help undergraduates understand the institution of higher education as compared with other social institutions. A few programs have stressed preparing scholars and teachers for programs in higher education. As we have indicated, such activity has not been promising, although one possible outcome may be the conceptualization of a way by which future scholars and professors can be prepared. We are not persuaded that the current informal ways scholars enter the field are either effective or efficient nor that current programs are worthwhile alternatives. Some better means of induction into the field ought to be found.

One absolute essential for any scholarly field is that it must satisfy some reasonably visible social and human needs so that the society will actually support it. Several criteria justifying its support have been variously met since World War II. First, does the research and scholarship satisfy the patron supporting the activity? Several foundations, the federal government, and, to some extent, state government have appeared to be sufficiently satisfied as to increase their support for research and scholarship. Recently a reaction may have set in as philanthropy and the federal government have turned away from supporting centers, institutes, or large-scale research studies. By 1973, this change in climate had produced something near panic in certain larger installations. The change of climate may ultimately force researchers and scholars to be more introspective about the values of their work and perhaps produce better evidence to persuade patrons that continued support is warranted.

Second, does it contribute to professional understanding of the field? For example, does intensive surveying of attitudes of college freshmen reveal more about the collegiate phenomenon than could be determined by an insightful journalist, sensitive counselor, or faculty adviser from casual contacts? Here the performance of research and scholarship in higher education reveals a decidedly uneven picture. Several surveys of statewide coordination seem to have unearthed much deeper understanding and, certainly, the findings of studies such as those sponsored by the College Entrance Examination Board of the success of American higher education in providing access transcend the casual observations of experienced observers. But other works seem to either overemphasize the obvious or become so preoccupied with specific detail or esoteric theory that they preclude understanding.

Third, does it produce people who can do the tasks the field implies? Since graduates of programs in higher education are placed in administrative positions and follow reasonably consistent career slopes in higher education administration, the field must be judged successful. However, how different these higher education graduates are from those who acquire similar positions through other means is a question that has not been answered. Hence, the verdict must be moot. As we have stressed repeatedly, the field has not succeeded in perpetuating itself in the form of younger scholars seriously addressing and publishing on important research topics. This may be because the field is new, with the majority of graduates still in their late thirties or early forties.

Fourth, does it produce more than a mere accumulation of facts? Each of the existing social and behavioral science fields has gone through a period of fact accumulation which contributed little to overall understanding or generalization. Gradually, as people involved increased, as financial support accelerated, and as heuristic or induced theory was used to interpret facts, fields such as sociology or social psychology attained scholarly maturity. One must observe that in 1973, the field of higher education had not gone beyond the raw accumulation of fact. Perhaps this is good. No science can proceed far unless there has been a good collection and classification of its phenomena as they exist in real life. An essential part of this criterion is that a field warrants support and preservation only when it presents a picture of logical, consistent accumulation of knowledge, which in aggregate presents a panoramic view that can be assimilated and acted upon by human beings.

Summary

A composite view of higher education as a field of study in current status is a contrast between the ideal and reality. If the ideal were realized there would be broad acceptance of programs and professors of higher education so that people would turn instinctively to them as sources for specialized knowledge. Within institutions the existence of highly competent, knowledgeable specialists in higher education would be recognized by all campus units. When study commissions are created, centers or departments for the study of higher education would automatically be turned to for necessary expertise or to obtain requisite knowledge. Also, ideally, there would be a systematic classification and storing of knowledge so that workers throughout the field would know what is known, what next should be known, and what are the workable strategies and tactics to gain that new knowledge. A recognized network of individuals considered standard setters could monitor work being attempted and judge the quality of proposed programs or the merits of individual candidates. While, by 1973, there is a cadre of reasonably well-recognized writers, scholars, and researchers, they possess neither the stature of, say, the membership of the National Academy of Sciences, nor the cohesiveness of leadership of the fields of history, mathematics, or physics. Ideally, there should be clearly recognized linkages between higher education and other applied fields with reciprocal rather than one-way relationships. Graduate schools of business and law should look to higher education for insight as well as providing insight to help the professional study of higher education. Also, practitioners should find some value in research whether it deals with junior college education, attrition of students, or the organization of student personnel offices.

Today higher education as a field of study is generally deficient in most of these ideal characteristics. It has not gained broad acceptance nor has it produced a systematic classification of knowledge. There are some visible scholars, but there is no clearly accepted group of arbiters, monitors, and standard setters. Linkages with other fields are for the most part unidirectional—higher education draws upon them but contributes little in return. Those in the field try verbally to describe their activity coherently and are defensive about relationships with other fields. The possibly premature formation of an association of professors of higher education is one index of this defensiveness, as are the efforts of graduate students to set themselves apart from other groups.

In addition, the research and scholarly achievements are spotty. Psychometrics (measurement, test development, evaluation) has produced a reasonable technology but failed to develop theoretical linkages to practice and has failed to demonstrate how consistent results can be used. Neither has it produced a technically competent group who continue to work in the psychometric examination of higher education. Only a handful of those active in the 1950s are still involved in psychometrics. The history of higher education has produced a few landmark synthesizing works but the linkages with history and other fields have been relatively weak. For example, several pioneering sociological studies of higher education were flawed because sociology was not linked with the forefront of historical research. Economics, apart from the work of several individuals, has been weak quantitatively, weak in linkage with other fields, and weak with respect to representation in the main core of the literature of higher education. Political science has made no substantial contribution to the understanding of higher education. Political scientists have produced a few descriptive works but have almost self-consciously indicated that they did so as journalists rather than as political scientists. Philosophy has contributed virtually nothing to the understanding of higher education; indeed, only one or two philosophers have actively cultivated the field. Anthropology represents truly virgin territory; it has contributed almost no one and no cluster of insights. And, overall, those working in higher educational research and scholarship have scarcely touched the power of mathematical or statistical analysis.

Higher education as a field of study may progress into a coherent, respected, discipline-like activity, comparable to medicine or it can remain a variegated cluster of interesting subjects studied almost idiosyncratically by individuals who accidentally found themselves on the terrain. Since institutions of higher education are made up of faculty and students who insist on involvement in decision-making and since ultimately the support of the general public is essential, the ultimate impact of higher education as a field of scholarly effort will depend greatly on sensing and influencing the values of individuals and groups by careful interpretation of research which, in itself, can never be definitive of policy.

Chapter Four

PROBLEMS AND ISSUES

Out of 870 graduates of doctoral programs in higher education at twelve universities with large and well-established programs, including UCLA, Florida State University, Indiana University, Michigan State University, the University of Michigan, the University of Washington, and the University of Wisconsin, 247 or 28 percent gave us comments and suggestions in response to a questionnaire survey we undertook of their views about their program. The majority of the respondents had specialized in administration; and 146 had earned the Ph.D., while 101 had earned the Ed.D.

Almost half of the respondents indicated neither dissatisfaction nor satisfaction with the features of their program. Dissatisfaction was most commonly expressed with language requirements and with required courses in the foundations of education. Both were viewed by many of the group as irrelevant to either understanding higher education or working in the field. In contrast, higher education core requirements, emphases in higher education, cognates outside of education, and the dissertation were generally approved.

Suggestions for strengthening the programs were wide-ranging but could be grouped readily into six categories: First, the largest number of respondents (121) advocated more practically-oriented experiences: internships; practicums; field work; management techniques; close contact with operating programs, community services, and legal and financial problems; and the use of visiting experts including recent graduates. Second, 81 of them focused on strengthening quality by eliminating weak programs; more selective admissions; continued review, periodic evaluation, and updating of programs; and adoption of more rigorous requirements and standards; with accreditation and certification as possible ways of accomplishing these goals. Third, 32 respondents noted inadequacies in research experience and called for better development of research skills, more experience in conducting and analyzing research, and courses in statistics, data processing, and computer programming. More emphasis on interpreting and using rather than on doing research was suggested. Fourth, 31 suggested that education course requirements be reduced and that the degree be made multidisciplinary by establishing bonds with other departments and by increasing the credits available for cognates. Fifth, improvement in the quality of faculty was suggested by 27, who mentioned inadequacies of advising, teaching, interest in students, and practical and recent experience in relevant aspects of higher education. And sixth, 24 called for clarification of program goals and purposes, including attention to skills in human relations and to ethical and moral standards for higher education.

Despite general approbation for dissertation experiences, several respondents also pointed to a lack of realism on the part of dissertation advisors in demanding either a theoretical basis for research, undue use of statistical analyses, or excessive rewriting of the dissertation to accommodate personal predilections as to forms of expression, organization, and treatment and presentation of data. Several others concerned with program quality mentioned a need to improve the image of the programs by wide dissemination of information, exemplary actions in respect to standards, and mutual cooperation among programs. Finally, the placement of degree recipients was also mentioned as requiring improvement, possibly by joint efforts of the programs.

The vast majority of those responding to our question as to

what they would do differently if they were to plan their degree program on the basis of their present knowledge indicated that they would make no significant change. Some thought that they had wasted time in taking an unnecessary number of courses, while others would add practically-oriented courses (finance, management, research, and so forth) to their original program. A significant number regretted not taking more courses outside of education, either as cognates directly related to the higher education program or simply in an academic discipline having some possible relevance to phases of higher education study or administration. Several expressed regret that they had taken an Ed.D. which their experience indicated was widely regarded as second rate compared with the Ph.D.

In general, these responses reinforce most of the doubts, concerns, and conclusions which we had already developed from our observation and review of programs; from faculty, students, and alumni interviews; and from our general conception of the nature of graduate professional education. Although our own judgments of doctoral programs in higher education are somewhat subjective, impressionistic, and by no means applicable to all of them, we detect a number of weaknesses in purposes, personnel, program content, student selection, and program evaluation.

Purposes

The first need, repeatedly emphasized in interviews, letters, and open-ended comments on our survey, is for clarification and restriction of purposes. What type of personnel should be prepared in higher education programs: teachers, administrators, researchers, service and public relations personnel, or (both a more limited and a broader conception) those individuals who have potential to become the distinguished professional educators of the future? Should higher education programs be advertised as the appropriate route to become a president, dean, or department chairman? If the preparation of researchers is a major goal, what emphases should be encouraged? To what extent should graduate students from other disciplines elect courses or plan minors in higher education? (Valuable as this particular prospect appears to be, marked increase in that service role will greatly increase faculty load, detract attention from the degree program, and diminish faculty time for research.) To what extent should the higher education faculty undertake chores for the university, such as program evaluation, needs surveys, planning, institutional research, confidential advice to the president, studies for committees or other departments and colleges, special courses for undergraduates, evaluation of faculty services, and so forth? (One view is that all requests for assistance should be honored, since failure to do so may interfere with development of cordial relations and additional resources; another is that uncritical assent is the sure road to overload and mediocrity.)

Admittedly, formal programs in higher education are products only of the last several decades, and the parameters of the field are still being established. Thus there is yet no general agreement as to answers to such questions of aim and objective as these, nor to the dimensions and scope of the study of higher education at large. But such questions should be resolved before faculty members are hired and students are admitted to a new program, for the answers have implications for faculty and student selection and, indeed, for the total structure and placement of the program. Instead, a number of universities have entered the field of higher education in a quite casual way and appear to have little understanding even within their schools of education as to the rationale for their higher education program and the careers for which it should prepare people.

Reality becomes almost a caricature when a team from a school of education decides there should be an emphasis on higher education, recruits a professor to head the program, then writes to the few visible departments elsewhere for bibliographies, syllabi, and advice as to what a department of higher education should do—all, apparently, without consideration of these fundamental and preliminary issues of purpose. Soon the program exists; it has students; its graduates get jobs; but no one knows what it should accomplish or what it should become.

Personnel

Many of the most visible contributions of research on higher education have been made by persons without formal training or fulltime positions in the field. Thus David Riesman began as a sociologist, Clark Kerr as a labor economist, and Seymour Harris as an economist; and such men have generally produced their work not from a department of higher education nor from discipline-based departments in schools of education but rather from a para-educational bureaucracy or an interdisciplinary center for research. At the same time, professors in departments of higher education have not published a substantial body of comparable research. Many of them do considerable consulting and contract survey work and, of course, teach their courses; they talk at length about research in higher education; and they write for university house organs and association newsletters—but they contribute little to the mainstream of literature concerning higher education.

It may be that the very nature of programs in higher education in schools of education simply do not attract research-oriented or research-qualified individuals. Such a phenomenon is certainly consistent with other patterns in schools of education whose faculties, except in a few institutions, have not been particularly productive of research. However, the rationale of the American Ph.D. degree is that it prepares students to do research in their chosen field; and this logically presupposes research competency by those directing their work.

Some institutions have entered the field of higher education by appointing individuals unacquainted even with the scholarship that exists, let alone with research methodology. We are frequently solicited by individuals who have been appointed as professors of higher education and who want to know what comprises the domain and what should be its program components. One large mid-western state university, for example, searched some eight years for a department head in higher education, and finally chose an assistant to the president of a West Coast institution who had had no formal or systematic contact with higher education as a field of study. His immediate reaction was to spend a full day with one of us, obtaining bibliographies, names of active scholars, and ideas as to how a program should be organized and to what ends. Another institution hired a former dean of students, a former community college president, and a former director of adult education for a higher education faculty and expected them to begin immediately to direct doctoral-level thesis research, when nothing in their professional backgrounds since completing their own theses qualified them for this task. Other examples abound of individuals who, after years in business education or adult education or even secondary school administration, suddenly become professors of higher education and offer courses supposedly appropriate for doctoral students. These factors tend to give a number of programs a distinctly amateur quality and their courses a manifestly anecdotal flavor. Former administrators may have had many experiences of interest to aspiring administrators, but these come to make up much of course time not already consumed by parttime students engaging in "show and tell" about their own ongoing administrative problems and experiences.

Several reasons can be advanced for this problem of inadequate faculty. One is that some programs have been created with the hope that somehow they could help improve the process of higher education without the need for basic understanding of it. In this connection, one large state university program consisting of seven fulltime equivalent faculty members and well over 100 students may be typical. Its department head explained that his faculty was using the results of scholarship rather than undertaking their own research in order to provide advanced education for leaders in a region dreadfully deficient in educational leadership. He argued that it was better to use the state's resources in this way than for faculty members to be preoccupied with their own research and scholarship. The students themselves, however, saw things differently. They were reasonably pleased with their courses and their internship experiences, but they were poignant in their desire for at least a leavening of actively producing scholars on the faculty.

A second rationale is that the situation may be transitory, in that higher education as a new field may simply be following in the footsteps of other fields or scholarship. Dale Wolfle (1972, p. 5) illustrates the earlier professionalization of science with this incident:

> In 1802, Benjamin Silliman became the first professor of chemistry at Yale. There were then only 21 other full-time scientific positions in the United States (Daniels, 1968, pp. 13–14), and the professional requirements for most of those few positions were modest. Professors were hired to teach the science that was already known—to add to that knowledge was not ex-

pected, as the condition of the Yale appointment indicated. In 1801, Silliman was a 22-year-old law student contemplating accepting a teaching position in Georgia. One warm July morning he met Timothy Dwight, Yale's president and an old family friend and told him of the Georgia offer. Dwight immediately advised him to decline. Dwight said he should not voluntarily go to a part of the country in which slavery was practiced; the climate was dangerous and besides there was an additional reason. Yale had decided to appoint a professor of chemistry and natural history. No one in the United States was available and qualified; a foreigner, "with his peculiar habits and prejudices . . . [might] not act in harmony with his colleagues" (Reingold, 1964, p. 3). But if Silliman cared to become a chemist, he could have the position. The offer was welcome, even a relief, for Silliman was really not much interested in law. So he became a chemist within a year, going first to Philadelphia— America's scientific capital—and then on to Europe for some quick repairs to his scientific deficiencies.

Just as the nineteenth century was for science a period, in Wolfle's words, "of transition from the gentlemen amateurs who predominated in the eighteenth century to the professional scientist of the twentieth," so the present decades may be a similar period for the study of higher education. Programs in this field may currently be in an early state, manned by amateurs or people retrained from other fields, engaging in teaching what is known, or beginning to collect data for rudimentary taxonomic studies. If the field continues to mature, the present paucity of producing scholars could probably be over, following this example, in the 1990s.

A third reason is that there is no clear agreement as to the expertise which a professor of higher education should possess, and thus little assurance that potential professors from within the field have particular expertise. For example, at Stanford, which has the only named chair of higher education in the country, the search committee for a successor to the first incumbent, W. H. Cowley, passed over all candidates closely identified with the emerging study of higher education and selected instead a well-known political scientist/sociologist, James G. March, who had had three years of collegiate administrative experience and was just beginning a study of college presidents.

In comparing higher education with law, medicine, and other better established fields, professors of these other professions (with some recent exceptions, when people from other disciplines have been brought into these programs for special purposes) are generally expected to have been trained and credentialed within these professions. The medical degree or the law degree, for example, is presumed necessary to provide the essential skill and knowledge to teach and do research in these fields. No such assumption yet applies in the teaching or study of higher education.

Some believe that university programs in higher education are incapable of preparing future scholars in the field. This fear seems warranted in view of the relatively few graduates of these programs who are active scholars as well as teachers. But this fear, and the related problems of low visibility and respect that higher education programs share with other new or marginal fields of study, such as graduate programs in international affairs, ethnic studies, or policy analysis, do not seem to stem necessarily from the nature of the field. It may stem as much from the reliance of higher education on the casual drift of research workers from other activities into its teaching positions; and if this trend continues, the field may well have reached its zenith.

Admittedly heterogeneity of faculty background can be a source of strength to a department. But if programs in higher education continue to recruit as professors persons who have been disappointed or grown old in administrative ranks, or marginal professors in disciplinary departments who find teaching about teaching an effective surrogate for disciplinary scholarship, or other education faculty who find their original specialties in professional education no longer popular, such heterogeneity will ensure that the departments will retain permanently their present marginal status.

There are, of course, already exceptions to this pattern of recruitment, as, for example, in the program at Southern Illinois University, which as indicated in Chapter Two uses a large number of central administrative officers as adjunct or parttime professors and leaders of the program. But marginality will continue so long as letters for promotion or tenure of professors of higher education all too often read that while the candidate could not seriously be considered for promotion as a sociologist, economist, or political scientist, it might be permissible to promote him in higher education, since standards there are less rigorous than in these other departments.

What type of faculty should be sought or accepted for the higher education program? Ideally, those with some practical experience, some facility in analyzing and writing about higher education, and some unusual skill in teaching and in consultation with individuals. This ideal is not easily achieved. But according to graduates of higher education programs who responded to our questionnaire, four qualifications stand out. Competency and experience in teaching in the field of higher education was the most frequently desired, with practical experience in administration being second. Perhaps reflecting the administrative emphasis of the respondents, research productivity is specified as desirable by only half as many of them as successful experience in teaching and administration; but other comments demonstrate wide concern for knowing and understanding research on higher education. Fourth and finally, responses emphasized the importance of such personal qualities as the willingness to listen and flexibility in recognizing and adapting programs to the experience, interest, capabilities, and aspirations of individual degree candidates.

One final problem with personnel relates not to competency or background but to the fact that many programs in higher education have only one or at the most two professors assigned fulltime to them. Not only are demands on such faculty extraordinarily heavy, but the programs of necessity reflect the idiosyncratic emphases of these particular individuals. As examples, for almost a quarter century W. H. Cowley maintained a program in higher education at Stanford which reflected his own interests in a specific taxonomic mode of analysis and a highly personalized retrieval system to classify knowledge about higher education; and Earl J. McGrath's interest in liberal and general education gave a similarly distinctive flavor to the Institute of Higher Education at Teachers College. Both men produced capable graduates, but the intellectual base of their programs was so personalized that a sustaining intellectual foundation was never established to ensure the continuity of the programs' scholarly orientation. When these leaders departed, the programs were reoriented to conform to the interests of new incumbents. Certainly the interests of individual scholars and department heads should give some character or structure to their program, but in the more established fields there is a solid base which ensures that the department will be much the same in respect to the most important dimensions of the program, regardless of individual faculty members.

Content

The major weakness of higher education curricula center on course content. Our evidence is more impressionistic here than with previous problems, but based on talking with students in a half dozen of the larger programs, examining course syllabi, and through inference from samples of qualifying or preliminary examination questions, our impression is that many of the courses offered in programs of higher education are merely descriptive and frequently overemphasize current issues. Thus a course on the community college may describe its history and argue its significance and then describe a number of current issues facing junior college education. Courses on administration may discuss the historic role of boards of trustees; enumerate the responsibilities of presidents, deans, and the like; describe the evolution of the concept of shared responsibility; and then list the current issues facing academic governance.

Except for courses on the history of higher education which adopt a chronological framework, courses rarely appear to present a consistent framework or a consistent set of theoretical presuppositions. In part this reflects the descriptive quality of much of the available literature, and it obviously reflects the fact that, as a young field of study, the basic descriptive data on higher education is still being collected. Thus courses seem to serve primarily as means to channel this growing amount of descriptive information into the minds and notebooks of graduate students. Perhaps indicative of the current-events emphasis of courses, our experience from talking with graduate students across the country suggests that the *Chronicle of Higher Education* has for too many become their primary reference tool and the primary shaper of their opinions as to what is significant.

A related reason is the lack of theory in higher education. While many have yearned for it, there has grown up no generally accepted theory about how higher education functions, nor has there evolved a theory of how to study it. W. H. Cowley spent over a quarter of a century hammering out a method of analysis which has been used by his own doctoral students but has gained virtually no acceptance elsewhere. Nevitt Sanford and Joseph Katz based their thinking on a concept of developmental psychology first elaborated by Erik Erikson, but then they became quite eclectic when they started to write about it. Burton Clark, James March, and J. Victor Baldridge have begun to apply organizational theories to higher education, but as yet these theories have not gained wide use. In general, few professors of higher education are preoccupied with theoretical concerns. This being true, it is perhaps not unexpected that the most significant research seems to have come not from departments of higher education but out of nonuniversity centers such as the Carnegie Commission, Educational Testing Service, the College Entrance Examination Board, the American College Testing Program, the American Council on Education, UNESCO, a few offices of institutional research such as at the University of Minnesota, Michigan State University, and the University of Wisconsin, and an occasional academic department.

Higher education as a field of study embraces so many different subjects—governance, teaching, finance, personnel work, counseling, testing, and the like—that it fits well with no single theoretical base as does medicine with the biological sciences and social work with sociology and psychology. If a base ever is to be established, it will have to be an interdisciplinary one. Yet there are few indications of any serious attempt to contrive such a base. One such effort took place in the school of education at Stanford during 1973, when a group of economists, sociologists, political scientists, historians, lawyers, and representatives of the graduate school of business tried to hammer out a curriculum which would rest on a consistent interdisciplinary core of theory data. (The final report of their effort will be published late in 1974, authored by Lewis B. Mayhew.) The group was hopeful but not overly sanguine that it can succeed. Similar efforts ought to be attempted in other universities and by some of the organizations associated with higher education if an appropriate background for scholarship is to emerge.

A related weakness which may be simply the product of the developmental period of the field is the overelaboration of courses in the light of existing scholarship. In the voluminous literature concerning higher education, there is such enormous redundancy that we are forced to the conclusion that existing knowledge cannot really support more than a handful of courses. Probably there is enough scholarship to underpin one historical course, one dealing with types of institutions, one on governance and organization, one on the full range of personnel services including evaluation, and possibly one on contemporary college students—although much of the latter material is dated and restricted to the atypical student dissent of the 1960s. Other courses seem generally to be idiosyncratic variations on these few themes or eclectic montages drawn from their domains.

The needed and supportable courses in higher education can thus be taught by a relatively few faculty members. To extend this number of courses is to repeat the proliferation of relatively soft courses in professional education which took place during the 1930s, 1940s, and 1950s, and brought down on the heads of professional educators a storm of criticism led by Arthur Bestor, James B. Conant, and James Koerner. Similar proliferation of courses has occurred elsewhere in the university during the twentieth century, but at least in a few of these fields the new knowledge has expanded sufficiently to support additional offerings. In higher education, however, courses have increased much more rapidly than has knowledge or theory. This is especially true with respect to administration, where most of the existing theory and writing has dealt with government, business, or public schools and has very limited application to higher education. This proliferation may be transitory, in that new courses lacking an appropriate scholarly base may generate questions which will stimulate inquiry and thus lead to an expansion of knowledge. But for that to happen, faculty members and their students will need to reorient their efforts more distinctly toward research and scholarship.

One area where courses and degree requirements have been

insufficient rather than overextended is in quantitative skills, especially in view of the significance of quantification for many researchable problems. As was indicated in Chapter Two, a few programs do require a single course in statistics, but this is likely to be more descriptive—in that students learn to define *median, mode, standard deviation,* and similar terms, and perhaps learn to compute correlations—rather than one designed to develop competences for experimental research, model building, and computer simulation. It is, of course, difficult to document, but our contacts with students lead us to believe that candidates in higher education have been underprepared in mathematics as compared with those in the arts and sciences. A program which did not stress quantification could still be reasonably effective for preparing these students for administration, if not research, as long as administrative practice did not require quantification; but it is becoming apparent that higher education management and administration will require competencies in quantification just as research and scholarship do. Until such time as the recommendation of the Carnegie Commission on Higher Education is accomplished, calling on high schools to require a full four years of mathematics, this weakness cannot be readily corrected among graduate students in higher education who have had no more than two or possibly three years of high school mathematics and who have not taken any mathematics or the equally important computer sciences as undergraduates, except through respectable courses in quantification in their doctoral programs.

In addition to this quantitative weakness of many higher education programs, there are some marked deficiencies in those programs which aim essentially to prepare administrators. As implied above, the nature of higher education administration and management are changing rapidly, widening the gap between preparation and practice. Higher education catalogs, for example, list some courses on the financial management of higher education, uses of the computer, and decision-making, but these courses are in a distinct minority as compared with more descriptive historical or current-issues courses. Students may be able to take such work outside the school of education in schools of business administration or other departments, since the requirements for courses within education do not prevent elective courses outside education; but our conversations with higher education students in a number of institutions leads us to conclude that substantial training in business, finance, and management science is still the exception rather than the rule.

Most administrative programs also seem to ignore or assign relatively modest attention to preparation for long-range planning. Again, this is not a deliberate error; it reflects the recent and still quite primitive state of educational planning. The Society for College and University Planning is in an almost continuous state of identity crisis over who is actually involved in planning and how such persons should be prepared; and within institutions themselves there is little agreement as to organization, tactics, or strategies for planning and only scattered evidence of much actual planning beyond the next year's budget. Nonetheless, the significance of planning increases each year on the agenda of administrators; and programs preparing people for these roles might be expected to develop, adapt, or borrow courses to develop needed competencies.

Still another emerging concern which has received relatively little curricular emphasis is the relationship of higher education to law. For years the courts adopted a cautious posture with respect to the internal functioning of collegiate institutions, and campuses were governed more by broad principle and value statements than by written prescriptions and procedures ensuring due process. All this, of course, has been changed. Relations between collegiate institutions and students, staff, and faculties have been increasingly delineated by courts and legislation and structured on campus by constitutions, bylaws, formal judicial systems, and mechanisms to guarantee procedural rights. Dealing of both public and private institutions with state and federal governments are increasingly governed by administrative ruling or legislated law, as the Higher Education Amendments of 1972 illustrate in requiring state officials to distribute federal funds for higher education.

Such developments would seem to require in-depth exposure of future administrative officers to legal questions, concerns, and approaches in a much broader and sophisticated way than the earlier courses on school law for school principals and school superintendents. Yet for the most part such courses are not listed. Nor, with an exception or two, are there supportive relationships between a school of education and a school of law. Except for brief exposure to a few legal landmarks, such as the Dartmouth College case, students in higher education thus receive little training in legal issues or sensitivity.

Nor are matters of unionism, collective bargaining, and contract negotiations generally explored. This deficiency is underscored by the plaintive plea of a Stanford graduate who, six weeks after assuming a new post as academic vice-president, found himself in the midst of contract negotiations with absolutely no preparation for the tangled issues of campus unionism. While it is impossible to tell how widespread collective bargaining is likely to become on campus, the fact that unionism and collective bargaining characterize the higher education systems of the nation's largest states and cities suggests that administrators and managers must be increasingly prepared to deal with such questions. Our impression is that in only a few programs, such as the State University of New York at Buffalo, has the faculty made specialized studies of collective bargaining and included the results in the curriculum. Some programs may steer students to courses in the business school, the law school, or labor economics; but catalogs, questionnaires, and interviews do not reveal this as a frequent or salient practice. Thus while unionism is a powerful force which should be studied in degree programs, so far it is not.

Beyond these weaknesses in administrative preparation, one final curricular issue remains: that of desirable specialization. How much specialization should be encouraged, permitted, or even tolerated? If preparation of administrators is accepted as a responsibility, what specialties should be included: general, academic, financial, student personnel, admissions, records, residence halls, research administration, planning, and coordination? And should specialization be permitted to extend to immediate job openings such as coordinator of student activities, public relations director, budget analyst, or health sciences administrator; or should emphasis be on the interaction of students, faculty, administrators, and others within the context of an academic environment and the relation of this environment to the larger society?

If teacher preparation is accepted as a purpose, what teaching fields should be included: higher education, teacher education, or even undergraduate teaching (especially at the lower division) in all disciplines? And should advising and counseling, evaluation and testing, and educational technology be viewed as essential experiences for teachers or regarded as additional and separate specialties?

Based on answers to these questions, what type of organization should be adopted: A composite department within education, including higher education and other related fields such as administration, teacher education, adult education, and student personnel? A separate multi-focus department of higher education including administration, research, and teaching? Several specialized departments with these foci within higher education? A university-wide department, institute, or center drawing staff from the entire institution? Or two separate centers: an instructional unit, and an independent one for research and service?

It is unlikely that consistent answers will be found for any of these questions; but a common weakness of most programs is that extrinsic conditions, personalities, aspirations, and available resources have led to answers that have little to do with an analytical and rational consideration of alternatives and their implications. If anything, the tendency of programs has been in the direction of overspecialization and fragmentation, according to the graduates who responded to our questionnaire. A number of them favored a broad-issue and scholarly-oriented program and asserted that preparation for any specific position in higher education would be highly undesirable. Scholarship and a broad overview of higher education as a basis for understanding and judgment were seen by these individuals as the basic and primary goal of higher education programs. Consistent with the respondents' own specialty, administration in higher education was listed as an appropriate specialization more than three times as frequently as any other. Only four additional specialties were indicated as desirable by as many as 40 respondents —teaching of higher education, student personnel, institutional research, and business management. Only a few suggested special preparation for government agency or state board positions; and particularly interesting, no one at all advocated preparation for teaching subjects other than higher education.

Student Selection

The sheer size of some of the more visible departments of higher education leads us to suspect that many programs enroll far too many students and graduate far too many doctoral candidates considering their relatively few fulltime faculty members. This judgment is made partly by comparing the productivity of large graduate departments in arts and sciences with those in higher education and partly out of our own conviction as to the amount of time and attention required fully to prepare Ph.D. recipients.

One factor which underlies this problem is the nature of financing programs in higher education. Although a few programs do offer undergraduate courses, the great majority provide only master's and doctoral level courses, which by their nature enroll relatively few students. Thus they have no large mass of undergraduate students to help underwrite the graduate seminars, as do most academic departments. Programs lodged in schools of education which have substantial undergraduate enrollments can sometimes avoid this difficulty; but in schools serving primarily graduate students the problem becomes acute. If the programs do not generate sufficient course enrollments, central administration becomes skeptical that fulltime faculty should be allocated to them, particularly since there may be some uncertainty as to what they actually contribute to the institution. To placate such criticism there may be a temptation to enroll more graduate students than can be comfortably accommodated in truly rigorous doctoral level training. Thus we find it appalling rather than praiseworthy when a single thesis advisor produces as many as eight doctorates in one year.

A second weakness is the tendency for many programs to enroll disproportionately large numbers of parttime students. Parttime enrollments is clearly a means to upgrade educational workers, particularly for credentialing purposes; and parttime study is clearly the easiest way for graduate students to support themselves financially. But one can raise the question as to whether or not parttime attendance can provide the deep immersion which seemingly is required to prepared scholars or well-inculcated professionals. Apparently successful efforts of graduate departments in the sciences to prepare future scientists has involved the immersion of graduate students as fulltime students in course work, research assistance, and even postdoctoral study. Law schools and medical schools have produced distinctive modes of thought on their students largely through similar immersion. The tightly prescribed first year of law school seeks to develop in students the capacity to think like lawyers and to think of themselves as lawyers, and the full four years of medical school have the same objective in medicine. It is doubtful that parttime involvement in programs of higher education can accomplish such a scholarly or professional socialization. The data, of course, are not yet available. Yet the hypothesis can be advanced that programs which cater to parttime students will generally upgrade the credentialed level of the positions these students occupy but will never come to be regarded as the principle source either for high-level administrative leadership or for scholarship. Certainly it seems unlikely that parttime students will become the leading professors of higher education of the future.

The scenario of graduate study which we believe to be all too typical is for students to matriculate in programs of higher education and to attend courses on a parttime basis until entitled to sabbatical leave from their institution. During their sabbatical, they satisfy residency requirements, pass preliminary or qualifying examinations, and begin the lonely quest for an appropriate thesis topic. Its discovery coincides with the end of the sabbatical, and they return home to develop their projects during evenings and weekends. From time to time they may return to the university for brief consultations with their advisors, although these meetings more frequently than not consist of reporting on progress rather than working together to solve difficult substantive problems. Generally, because of the number of advisees, these parttime candidates flow through the system and graduate or disappear with minimum critique or assistance from their advisors.

Such a system opens the way for clear abuse with no procedural devices to prevent abuse, while these in charge may loudly proclaim its virtues of practicality and reality. Lacking any safeguards, there is a tendency to admit persons neither qualified for nor interested in doctoral work—especially when the individual has held a teaching or administrative position for some years in a nearby college, a state office, or elsewhere within the university itself. Concern about admissions is voiced by some professors with high standards who criticize some of their colleagues; others recognize and rue their own tendency to give every applicant a change; and all too often the master's degree is viewed as the way out of a bad choice.

Evaluation

The last major problem derives from the rapid growth of programs in higher education. Because both a need and a demand seem to exist for their products, programs have proliferated swiftly with little if any quality control on the part of universities themselves, regional accrediting associations, or organizations concerned with higher education. Specialized accreditation is probably not the answer to this need, for the growth of specialized accrediting agencies in other fields has already placed an enormous burden on universities while seemingly not reducing the number of inadequate programs. Yet quality control could be undertaken by institutions themselves or by systems of institutions. An example of what can be done was the recent review of the program in higher education at the State University of New York at Buffalo under the auspices of the graduate dean, where three recognized outside scholars were brought to the campus, furnished a great deal of information, and asked to judge the quality of the staff, students, and program. This kind of institutional introspection seems the most hopeful way of dealing with quality control, at least for the time being.

The need for some type of external assessment has been dramatized by a new doctoral institution in one state of the union that has been created by an "all but dissertation" candidate at one of the more visible higher education programs in another state. Applying all of the procedures of his former university, this student organized a degree-granting institution which is a caricature or even a travesty on graduate work in higher education—one that epitomizes all of the weaknesses reviewed in this chapter. His institution requires candidates to possess a master's degree and to have had at least three years of educational work experience. Those admitted spend five weeks the following summer taking courses and developing a dissertation topic. They then return to their own jobs and, working with a thesis director of their own choosing, finish a thesis. The next summer they spend two more weeks on campus taking courses, standing for their oral examinations, and receiving their Ph.D. degree in higher education. With such an arrangement, a small cadre of three fulltime administrative officers, a small parttime summer-school faculty, and some poorly remunerated parttime thesis directors handled 85 doctoral candidates the first year and anticipate an average of 250 graduates a year after the institution is in full operation.

We are not contending that the established programs in higher education have reached or are even approaching such a caricature, but we do suggest that the poorly defined purposes, less than adequate faculty, superficial programs, and excessively large enrollments of some of them suggest tendencies in this direction. It is up to the leaders of programs of higher education and their own universities to counter these tendencies through better evaluation and quality control if higher education as a field of study is to mature beyond marginality.

Chapter Five

TOWARD
NEW MODELS

*I*n previous chapters we have analyzed background developments in American higher education which have led to the development of higher education programs. We have analyzed the features of these programs, commented on their strengths and weaknesses, and identified a number of questions and issues for resolution. Discussion of the state of research in higher education and its components as a scholarly field points up additional problems and brings us to consider the need for and the factors involved in developing new models for higher education programs.

New Goals

A discussion of new models must begin by specifying what they are to accomplish. Existing models for doctorates in higher education, although innovative because they offer a new specialization have been markedly limited because of the tradition that a doctorate is a departmental degree. Hence the most common, if not actually the preferred, path has required a department of higher education or its equivalent. Since *education* is prominent in this designation, the natural tendency is to imbed the program and department in the college of education. Faculty do not always accept this as desirable, although there seems no strong inclination to seek alternatives.

One result of this association is that certain characteristics are encouraged or enforced by it; specialties and requirements are defined as much by expediency as by a statement of intent. A department or a degree typically requires a viable size and sufficient interest among faculty and administrators. As a result, such departments may include adult education, teacher education (teachers of teachers), community college teaching, undergraduate teaching, counseling, student personnel work, administration, institutional research, and evaluation, as well as education of researchers and professors of higher education. No doubt courses, seminars, or experiences yielding insight into higher education are desirable for persons interested in these fields. Yet, were scholars of higher education to objectively examine these disparate specialties, it is doubtful that they would agree that all can be effectively accommodated in a single program. However, they might agree that a common core of two or three should be prescribed or that a somewhat larger group of courses be made available on an elective basis.

Educators concerned with adult, continuing, or lifelong education typically are committed to an organizational pattern parallel to, rather than a part of, traditional structures. They see education as less disciplinary-based and more related to the needs and interests of adults, as encompassing immediate recreational, vocational, and social concerns, and hence requiring somewhat different courses and instructional patterns. External degree programs and other nontraditional approaches may make this characterization less apt. But at the moment, credence must be given to their views.

Community colleges are still so new and insecure that programs in administration (and to a lesser extent, teacher preparation) must be directly related to them, while enthusiasm and commitment are fostered. Courses distinctive in designation if not in content in administration, finance, curriculum, personnel work, and instruction are often regarded as essential. Though not convinced of either the necessity or validity of the contention, we understand and sympathize with the motivation. But such courses are neither challenging nor appropriate for those interested in the total higher education enterprise. We have also found that the student specializing in the community college may be uncomfortable in courses in which students with a broader orientation predominate.

Institutional research requires such a range of knowledge and proficiencies that the typical higher education program may be the least desirable preparation. The intelligent institutional researcher can quickly learn on the job most of what he needs to know about higher education problems. What he basically requires is some understanding and sympathy with academic aspects of the university and sufficient skill in the use of analytical techniques to present data that will provide greater insight into university operations and thereby contribute to wiser decisions.

The traditional preparation for college teaching has been the Ph.D. in a discipline. Despite its irrelevance and weaknesses for teaching when strictly defined, the Ph.D. may still be preferred by those who do not wish their career delimited by the degree acquired. Unless a more flexible approach is established the D.A. may become more widely available and acceptable for those primarily desirous of a career in undergraduate teaching. If so, it should and will be regarded as more appropriate than a degree in higher education, however flexibly defined. This may ultimately be true for the community college as well as four-year colleges and universities.

In any case, higher education programs are not, in our judgment, the appropriate place to prepare college teachers in the disciplines, though they may well offer the best possible means of preparing professors to offer higher education courses in institutions catering to the broad range of clientele listed above.

The Massachusetts Institute of Technology has recently announced a program whereby a student once accepted in a departmental doctoral program may request an interdepartmental committee and plan a program incorporating study in several disciplines and preparation for college teaching, including appropriate experiences in higher education courses, teaching internships, and an atypical dissertation. In a few universities, the D.A. program has been developed to a point where courses in curriculum and instruction in the discipline, a few higher education courses, a teaching internship, and an instructional or curricular dissertation are molded into a unified experience. Extension of the D.A. program to an interdisciplinary emphasis is also possible. Either of these models offers a sounder basis for preparing college teachers than does a higher education degree. The reasons are at least threefold. First, a disciplinary-based degree presents fewer hazards to a teaching career for a person who may begin in a community college or liberal arts college, but who ultimately aspires to a university appointment; second, the level of generality of higher education courses relating to teaching or curriculum development usually makes them less applicable to teaching a particular discipline than do related courses provided under the auspices of that discipline; third, the number of higher education (or education) courses relevant to a teaching career in a discipline is usually far less than the number required for a degree in higher education, thus permitting greater depth in the discipline. A few well-planned courses in higher education can make a significant contribution to the preparation of college teachers. That is a desirable and sufficient role.

The preparation of student personnel workers relates to a segment of the university which today has only indirect relationship to the major purposes of higher education. Personnel workers are facilitators rather than direct contributors. Those who seek administrative careers in this field are as well or better prepared in departments of psychology as in education. They require experiences in counseling, personality development, financial aids, residence halls, student activity supervision, admissions, and health. These interests and needs may be much more akin to those of social workers than to academic administration or college teaching. We regret the lack of academic orientation and understanding in many student personnel programs and believe that a higher education program might provide a superior education for some student personnel workers, but the typical candidate in the field is unfortunately disinterested in courses covering instruction, curriculum, finance, research, statistics, history, learning, and academic administration. There is apparently more in common among student personnel work in secondary schools, colleges, and universities than there is between student personnel work and the broader concept of higher education. Thus our model for student personnel workers would associate them with educational psychology, counseling psychology, clinical psychology, or social work. This, of course, does not deny the worth of a few higher education courses in such a program; in fact, two or three should be strongly recommended.

Similarly, we doubt that higher education programs are an appropriate site for teaching content or methods courses required for secondary or elementary teaching in a particular discipline. Though they will be in college or university departments, perhaps jointly in a disciplinary department and an education department, their ultimate focus is on lower levels of education. Again, a few selected courses in higher education may provide background, but their major experience should come from faculty in the substantive discipline and education faculty engaged in teacher preparation— likewise, a department of higher education is clouded by faculty specializing in teacher education for the lower levels of education. If higher education should not undertake to prepare college teachers in the substantive disciplines surely it should not include those oriented to lower levels, either.

The relative value of inherited traits, longtime personal development, and specific education for success in any task will never be known with certitude. Physical characteristics (surely inherited in part) may be more important than previously realized. Being male, attractive in personality, above average in height, socially adept, and having a sonorous and pleasant voice are certainly not disadvantages in becoming a college president. An attractive wife may help, too. Perhaps in the past a candidate with a definite program for reorganization of a college was attractive to a board, but as faculty and students have become involved in presidential choice, their aspirations may favor a person who speaks adroitly but ambiguously about upholding traditions, achieving excellence, and involving all parties in decision-making. Some faculties and student bodies would prefer a custodian or caretaker rather than a policy maker, executive, or administrator. And a few boards of trustees agree. The effective administrator may be one whose personal goals are never revealed by his public statements.

The preceding remarks, are only in part facetious, suggesting that becoming a college president or dean requires considerably

more than a degree in administration. They also raise questions
about the content of a training program for administrators. It is
possible that cosmetics, a Procrustean stretching, and a concentrated
charm school experience might be as effective as anything else.

Exploration of Alternatives

In attempting to fulfill all of these specialties, programs in
higher education have responded to needs. No doubt they should be
complimented, especially since the traditional departmental commitment to the research oriented Ph.D. has long forbidden more
adequate responses. But the expediency of attracting students, increasing staff and courses, and developing a varied market has
surely been a major factor. Freed of such mundane concerns, we
shall examine in the remainder of the chapter some principles and
experiences designed to meet these needs in the best possible way.
The internship offers an attractive and flexible method for specific
experience and training in most of the specialties.

Five or six universities should have universitywide centers
that are devoted to the study of higher education but do not grant
degrees. True, the students attracted might include an undue proportion of misfits and rejects from the disciplines. But without the
degree program the burden of teaching and dissertation direction
would no longer usurp all resources and the center might thus
attract professors interested in applying their discipline to the study
of higher education, either individually or as members of an interdisciplinary team. Degrees in higher education, if any, would be
offered through the college of education. Center faculty might
conduct seminars, but they would be research-oriented at an advanced level. Alternatively, the center might offer seminars or lectures on research in various aspects of higher education, to both
faculty members and graduate students, with the latter granted
credit by arrangement with their departments. Indeed, it might be
wise to encourage professors associated with the center to develop
courses or seminars relating their own discipline to higher education, thus attracting more graduate students in the disciplines to
become aware of its direct application to higher education. Students
in education would undoubtedly benefit from contact with pro-

fessors and students from other disciplines, while avoiding the diluted, elementary approach sometimes found in courses like Economics of Higher Education which may be taught by a non-economist and elected by or required of students with little or no background in economics.

Students planning a career in research on higher education should have an internship of one or two years and produce a dissertation under the direction of a professor actively engaged in the field. In fact, the dissertation could and usually should be a natural culmination of the internship. Policies on the organization and style of the dissertation should be modified so that students completing a study, a significant portion of a study, or contributing a major though inseparable part of a study may have their work accepted without undue delay or extensive rewriting and processing. Team efforts in dissertations present problems, but should be permitted. Most students would receive a degree in a basic discipline and be equally qualified to teach in that discipline or join a department or center of higher education.

Centers for research on higher education should include the practical and the applied as well as the theoretical. Theory development has no value unless it can be applied to understanding the administrative process and predicting the success or failure of particular procedures. Hence persons actively and deeply engaged in institutional research should be affiliated with the center. The center can then use the institution as a laboratory and doctoral students can engage in live, immediately applicable studies to sense the problems involved in human reactions and in obtaining accord on a study or its recommended actions.

The role of internships in doctoral programs in higher education does not emerge clearly. Internships are generally recommended or available rather than required. Reading between the lines, one may conclude that an internship depends on the candidate's interest and the graduate adviser's predilections. The availability of satisfactory internships, time required, and credit are also factors. From personal experience and student and faculty comments, we conclude that few programs assign a sufficient bloc of credits to permit an individual to concentrate on the internship long enough to make it worthwhile. And we conclude that for a student to work out three credits of internship over a quarter or semester, along with two or three other courses, is an excessive drain on the person or office with which he interns, and that the value of the experience itself is questionable.

However, a properly planned internship can become a highly significant educational experience. It usually requires a minimum fulltime half year or halftime full year, and should be paid, so that the student accepts a professional obligation toward the assignment and the supervisor gains both a sense of responsibility and an expectation that the student will accept and fulfill assignments. In addition, a significant bloc of credits (12 to 20) should go with the task. Compared with the typical 0–5 credits, the number might seem excessive. However, by requiring readings related to the internship, the definition of a project based on it, and completion of a summary report or paper, the credits can easily be justified. Furthermore, the pattern corresponds to the thoughtful approach expected of an administrator especially educated for his career. We found no specific examples of this pattern but were told that it occasionally happens. We frankly do not understand the view that pay and credit must not be granted for the same task. Our view— pay is for the work done and credit is for what is learned—could even be interpreted as consistent with that faculty bias.

Some candidates for a Ph.D. in higher education are already employed in administration usually at the level of assistant dean or assistant to a dean or president. Should their experience qualify for internship? Should credit be granted for it? It depends on the nature and quality of the experience. If a candidate can demonstrate acquaintance with relevant concepts and principles of administration and show that his decisions and activities have been guided by conscious recourse to them, the experience, because it was *real,* may well be better than that provided in the university program. Appraisal will require time and effort and a committee decision based on interrogation of the candidate and evidence on his job peformance, else those with administrative experience will come to expect credit automatically. In current practice, it seems internships are primarily for those without administrative experience, yet credit is not given for prior experience. Apparently, and most unfortunately, prior experience, whether good or bad, is an acceptable alternative to an internship.

Many recipients of the higher education doctorate serve some sort of internship in the postdegree M.D. pattern. Those with limited prior experience frequently take initial positions as administrative assistants to presidents or other officers. Such positions usually, though not always, offer opportunity for an in-depth experience with administration, but in an observational and facilitative capacity. Some experiences, unfortunately, turn out to be little more than clerical paper-shuffling. The role of "assistant to" does appear to be a good stepping stone to line administrative positions, bypassing the teaching, committee service, and minor administrative assignments through which many deans and presidents usually progress. The move from assistant to the president to vice-president or even president in another institution is far easier than the traditional move through the ranks preferred by faculty, especially in large, top-ranking universities. Close association with a well-regarded college or university president apparently is expected to rub off on an assistant and provide within two or three years the equivalent of longer service in the traditional manner.

The training of faculty members through committee service, chairmanship, or service on ad hoc study committees, or task forces, or internships (or fellowships) of varying duration in the president's office also constitute recognized paths to administration. Clifton R. Wharton, Jr., president of Michigan State University, for a time provided foundation-supported fellowships for undergraduates, graduates, and junior faculty to observe and sometimes contribute to administrative decision-making through discussions and projects. Results have not been assessed and the reactions of the fellows varied from enthusiastic approval to doubts about its worth. A few years ago, the president of another state university selected two junior faculty members to serve as fellows, aides, or assistants in his office. Some grew disenchanted with administration, but admitted new insights and deep sympathy for the task. Others moved to administrative assignments.

The American Council on Education is currently in the tenth year of its Academic Administration Internship Program, designed to prepare carefully selected individuals for careers as deans, vice-presidents, or presidents of colleges and universities. The program has been eminently successful, although a careful evaluation would probably show that the selection as a fellow is at least as important as the subsequent experience in gaining entry to administration.

The Center for the Study of Higher Education at the University of Michigan, under the directorship of Algo Henderson, acquired funds for postdoctoral administrative fellowships which were also highly successful in identifying capable persons, providing an opportunity for study and experience in administration and subsequently moving to an administrative position.

In many respects, the postdoctoral fellowship has advantages over doctoral programs for the preparation of administrators. Doctoral specialization has little relevance in selection of postdoctoral programs, and doctorates in substantive disciplines other than education have some advantages for many administrative posts. The freedom from degree requirements, the status conferred by degree, fellowship, and previous faculty status create greater acceptability and open the door to greater involvement in the affairs of a university than predoctoral status. The combination of completed degree, fellowship status, and an introduction to administration surely provides superior background. However, this approach also has some disadvantages. It involves an additional year, and requires some source of funds to support the internships, especially since the participants must usually receive their full salary and even face additional expenses. The approach is not likely to meet demands for administrators but is a pattern which should be preserved and expanded if possible.

The programs and activities of the Institute of Higher Education of the University of Georgia exemplify a state or regional approach. Georgia's full range of programs includes some not specifically aimed at preparing administrators, yet all hold that potential. This institute is a service, instruction, and research agency organized to work with other institutions and agencies. Staff roles are advisory, consultative, informative, interpretative, and evaluative. Programs and activities include doctoral program in higher education—instruction and work experience for the preparation of personnel for positions of leadership. Internships arranged with presidents of appropriate institutions include fulltime participation at the host institution for one full quarter. Five to fifteen credits are granted. The host institution provides room and board and an expense stipend. The intern makes written reports at two-week intervals to the internship coordinator and is visited twice during the internship period. Final evaluation reports are required. The institute also offers management information and long-range planning for developing colleges, funded under the Education Professions Development Act to assist smaller institutions in the development of adequate information systems for purposes of long-range planning. It has programs for newly appointed administrators designed to provide inservice training and consultation for persons recently appointed to an administrative position in two-year or four-year colleges. Summer-scholar and academic-year fellowship programs are available to provide a general overview of higher education and to discuss the larger issues and problems with faculty members granted leave from developing institutions to continue their graduate education. It has a faculty development program that academically upgrades promising faculty members in Georgia's colleges and universities to fill leadership positions in their respective institutions. It sets up cooperative arrangements with other institutions and agencies for the purposes of program development, instructional improvement, and institutional evaluation and includes cooperative services for other units of the University of Georgia to assist in intercollegiate and interdepartmental activities for overall improvement of institutional effectiveness. Finally it publishes monograph and newsletter series to inform college administrators and faculty members of recent trends and developments in higher education and arranges conferences, seminars, forums, and workshops for specific purposes of improvement and development.

Although other higher education programs contain some of these features, the Institute at Georgia seems to have developed the most complete array of activities for training administrators in doctoral programs, providing postdoctoral experiences, and offering significant inservice training. The range of programs must surely add to the experience of the would-be administrators seeking a doctorate.

Apparently the Institute has also been successful in involving neighboring institutions in the program and in sharing its expenses. This, too, is worthy of emulation.

Specific Suggestions

Although we shall say more later about future directions for programs in higher education, some specific suggestions are appropriate in matters which we have quite seriously criticized. The principal weakness of academic programs in higher education is one of numbers, with the larger programs accepting too many candidates for the fulltime equivalent faculty. This judgment, of course, is based on certain assumptions regarding the nature of graduate education, and especially that of dissertation work. It is assumed that a fulltime faculty member will teach an average of two courses per term, whether the term is a quarter or a semester. It is also assumed that faculty time will be divided approximately between teaching and related activities, and research and scholarship. Some of the latter will necessarily involve field work and services. If this is a reasonable description of faculty time, then using the number of fulltime equivalent faculty as a planning statistic, an approximation of optimum enrollment can be developed. In a professional school, particularly when many dissertations involve intensive field work under supervision, two doctoral degrees per year is a reasonable average load for each fulltime faculty member. If candidates for degrees in higher education perform as do those in the arts or sciences, approximately 50 percent will drop out between matriculation and degree. Thus two candidates should be enrolled for every degree to be completed. This means that the primary capacity consideration is faculty time. A quite large fulltime faculty of six members, or 180 faculty/weeks of instructional commitment, could admit a maximum of about 10 doctoral students per year (but no masters students), a maximum of about 100 masters students per year (but no doctoral students), or any other combination representing a trade of 10 masters students for 1 doctoral student. For example, 20 masters students and 8 doctoral students could be admitted each year.

To visualize an optimum total program with the university

in a steady state consider that a six-member program might enroll in its first year 8 doctoral candidates and 20 masters candidates for a total enrollment of 28. The second year 28 new enrollments would be accepted, with 6 doctoral students now in their second year, for a total enrollment of 34. The third year would enroll 28 new students, with 6 doctoral students in their second year and 4 in their third year for a total enrollment of 38. Assuming a steady state for the program and assuming some variation in rates of progress, a fulltime equivalent faculty of 6 should have a stable total enrollment averaging between 36 and 42 students. This, of course, produces a student-faculty ratio of approximately seven to one which is obviously far lower than typical undergraduate student-faculty ratios, but one which is defensible if the claims about the expense of graduate work are indeed warranted.

Our data suggest that many programs shoulder a far heavier load but the combination of parttime faculty and parttime students and uncertainties about the extent of their involvement make even rough estimates impossible. Our load computations would lead to small classes unless course offerings at the doctoral level were severely restricted or attracted other students. Since courses in higher education are for the most part graduate level, no large lower-division pool of enrollments can offset these relatively small enrollments. In institutions experiencing financial stringencies, central administration may become concerned. However, several remedies might be attempted. The courses in higher education (since so many are descriptive and require no particular prior preparation) could be assigned course numbers to encourage nondegree enrollments; course descriptions and content could readily be modified to appeal to undergraduates, particularly those interested in the processes and nature of higher education. Departments in the sciences and arts might be persuaded to encourage more doctoral students to take a cognate field (or a course or two) in higher education, especially those preparing for teaching careers in colleges and universities. Similarly, enrollments could be built up if other professional schools were brought to see the values of higher education courses for their own students. And, of course, the actual enrollment in programs can be expanded numerically, as was indicated, by increasing the number of masters candidates while decreasing the number of doctoral candidates. This assumes that the master's degree is in no sense a research degree and that requirements are, for the most part, credit accumulation in specific courses. Obviously the faculty would wish to investigate the likely market quite thoroughly before embarking on a major change in recruiting.

Programs ought also to be quite parsimonious about claims made and distinct subspecialties offered. Our impression is that the better programs in higher education present a core of materials appropriate for a generalist, on the assumption that administrative specialization will likely develop later based on individual abilities and the condition of the market. To be sure, a few subspecialties have been developed programatically. Student personnel work, institutional research, and, ostensibly at least, junior college administration are the clearest examples. However, even those subspecialties on closer examination appear more generalist than technical. Within the student personnel domain counseling and testing appear to be the only professional activities which require considerable clinical experience and technical expertise in order to be adequately qualified. Programs in higher education might consider themselves as generalist preparation for those who will continue to do as they have in the past—gained specialized knowledge on the job—or who would develop specific expertise outside the school of education or within it if it maintained appropriate strength in a relevant specialty such as tests and measurements or counseling. Thus persons wishing to enter financial administration would obtain general preparation in departments of higher education and specialized preparation in a school of business. Outside fields which could also provide specialized training for higher education students include psychology, sociology, political science, economics, law, business, architecture, and engineering. Other relationships could be available for those with very specific career objectives, as for example the M.D. student who truly aspires to enter administrative work in medical education.

A third major recommendation is to reorganize the degree structure in higher education. As noted, some higher education programs offer the Ph.D., some the Ed.D., and some both. However, it is our impression that the differentiation between the degrees has become blurred and that the Ph.D. in higher education represents a compromise between the needs of aspiring administrators and the normal Ph.D. requirements, such as a genuinely research-based dissertation. Given the nature of departments of higher education and the future of their graduates, it might be better to refurbish the Ed.D. and make it more distinctly a program for practitioners. The final matter has to do with administrative lodging of programs of higher education. Colleges of education are not likely, of their own initiative, to give up higher education or move to make it an all-university program. At least two factors are involved. First, some higher education faculty feel threatened by the interests and special capabilities of faculty elsewhere in the university. Second, colleges of education are not likely to surrender any program while their resources are threatened by a surplus of teachers and tight budgets throughout higher education. Faculty members in other departments are generally not enthusiastic about affiliation with the college of education. At the same time, their interests are so restricted and diffuse that they provide no unified pressure for a universitywide instructional or research unit. Within colleges of education, the assignment or characterization of the higher education program is not likely to be determined by those who might prefer a separate department and a restricted role. Neither is the decision about the practitioner or research emphasis. Since the preparation of community college personnel through master's, certificate, or specialist programs has for several years been a major program in many universities, practitioner emphasis readily carries over to the doctorate.

There is no widely accepted rationale or pattern for the substructure of the college of education. The specialties attached to higher education or the fields joined with it to make a department are likewise decisions involving many persons and factors. Faculty members preparing teacher education personnel (who, in turn, ultimately prepare elementary and secondary school teachers) may prefer association with a graduate program in higher education rather than with elementary or secondary education. The same motivation may operate in guidance, tests and measurements, evaluation, and so forth. Thus prestige and aspirations may be more important than logic or models. A universitywide center or institute generally requires new funding since it exists outside the traditional departmental and college structure. Hence, the interest and support of central administration is usually essential. Thus the expectations of central administration and the disposition of the director are more likely to determine the emphases of the center and the relations with instruction. The decision to organize a center has often been interrelated with the desire to obtain the services of a person of established stature who, in part, dictates the conditions of his appointment. Heading a department with responsibility for a large degree program lacks the prestige and autonomy of directing a center or institute devoted to research on higher education. This emphasis and autonomy (plus a director with prestige) also makes the center more attractive for grants from foundations or the government. Centers, independent of the college of education and with funds to support research, are also in position to attract an interdisciplinary faculty. It is not surprising, then, that the autonomous research-oriented center or institute represent the prestige pattern of higher organizations to which many higher education faculty aspire and which many programs have attempted to emulate in name.

Components of Individual Programs

As for components and requirements for degrees, they are dependent upon the organizational pattern and the programs or specialties included. Universitywide requirements imposed on all graduate degree programs comprise the first level of determination and the requirements of the college of education the second. In a few universities, language requirements are still uniformly enforced for all Ph.D.'s, but may be waived for Ed.D.'s. In some cases, the Ed.D. is regarded as a professional degree administered entirely by the college of education. Sometimes the Ed.D. is the only degree available to the college of education and hence to higher education programs in the college. Usually the acceptance of transfer credits is determined by graduate school, and credits for informal educational or work experience or for practicums and internships by college or university policies. The acceptance of credits for courses outside of education may also depend on policies which apply to the program in higher education. The college of education often imposes core curriculum requirements on all doctorates. This combination of policies and requirements may greatly restrict the uniqueness and the individuality of the higher education program.

Research skills may be included as part of the higher education core or separately specified. In the latter, a wide range of research skills and courses may be offered: mathematics, statistics, sociological research or survey procedures, psychological research methodology, historical research, philosophical research, linguistic analysis, or a foreign language. Many of these courses fall outside education and could be regarded as part of a cognate or of a minor, but enrollment at an appropriate level may be discouraged by prerequisites, or by departmental attitudes.

In addition, the usual program is rounded out with a possible specialty in higher education, internships or practicums, and dissertation. One apparent reason why the credits alloted to internships and to the dissertation are sometimes minimal is that the requirements for core, research, and specialty account for such a large proportion of the total credits specified for the degree.

Greater flexibility could result from a somewhat different approach. One possibility could consist of several specialties and related sources of knowledge. An example might include backgrounds, including purposes, social role, dynamics, history, philosophy, psychology, and sociology; management including resource allocation and utilization, economics, finance, business management, accounting, systems analysis; and administration, including power, authority, bureaucracy, psychology, sociology, political science, and management.

A second approach specifies knowledge, research, scholarly skills and abilities involved in adding knowledge and developing theory, applied research and evaluation, and values underlying the higher education enterprise. Knowledge includes backgrounds (history, philosophy, sociology); current organization and operation, reports, surveys, problems; learning processes and goals (cognitive, affective, psychomotor, modes of learning and teaching, structure, concepts and methodology of the disciplines); management (resource allocation and utilization, economics, political science, accounting); and human factors (student characteristics and motivations, faculty characteristics and motivations, group interactions, reward systems and evaluation).

Research and scholarly skills and abilities include the research methodologies from the relevant disciplines and, in addition, may include operations analysis, factor analysis, linear programming, and other analytic methods usually dependent on the use of the computer.

Applied research and evaluation skills aimed at improving operations include accounting and auditing, program budgeting, cost effectiveness and cost benefit analysis, evaluation and improvement of the educational process for individuals, evaluation and improvement of educational organization and operation in relation to the needs of society and resources required, and study and improvement of the decision-making process.

The significance of knowing and internalizing the values underlying the higher education enterprise include primarily a sensitivity to and awareness of its social and individual benefits. These are implicit and occasionally explicit in the knowledge, research, and evaluation but too often either ignored or unrealistically expanded to mystical proportions so that a detailed analysis of economic considerations in the evaluation of the educational process becomes impossible.

These broader approaches to the development of individual programs underline the relevance of many disciplines and courses. In fact, even a limited compilation is impressive evidence of the interdisciplinary nature of higher education. Psychology includes psychological testing, social psychology, public opinion and propaganda, psychology of advertising, political psychology, individual differences, and attitude change. Educational psychology offers work in group processes, principles of behavioral modifications, psychology of adult life, programed learning, and theories of learning. Philosophy covers many concepts employed in description and explanation of human action and mental abilities. Relevant topics include philosophy of languages, scientific concepts, theory of knowledge, philosophical psychology, structure of science, moral philosophy, and social and political philosophy. Sociology covers such topics as methodology of the social sciences, sociology of formal organizations, and sociology of knowledge. Journalism or communications provides courses in the press and public affairs, administrative communications. In addition, relevant course offerings can be found in history, economics, speech, anthropology, business administration, political science and law.

Most of the preceding topics were suggested among alternatives available for cognates or minors in the higher education doctorate, but in some programs, attempts have been made to make higher education self-sufficient by using materials drawn from these various disciplines. This points up one of the most crucial issues regarding higher education programs. It can be posed in a series of questions.

Should higher education programs be based in the college of education or be provided under auspices making them more clearly interdisciplinary? Would higher education programs make a greater contribution by concentrating on a few basic courses and encouraging doctoral candidates in other disciplines to take a minor in higher education and apply their major discipline to its problems? Should higher education faculty be primarily drawn from basic disciplines or as it seems in several programs, should the staff consist of Ph.D.'s in higher education? Actually, the wording of these questions and the speculations about them suggest developments which are quite unlikely. Interdisciplinary programs are not easily developed in universities where the department continues to be the primary unit for offering courses and providing secure careers for faculty. Only faculty members of established stature can safely become involved on a continuing basis in such programs. The program may depend on one or two such persons and be severely weakened by their departure. Students, too, who venture into such interdisciplinary programs run the risk of jeopardizing their progress and ultimate careers by encounters with unreasonable requirements or by attempting to satisfy the various and sometimes conflicting views represented in a committee when a dissertation is presented.

Summary

Among existing programs we do find models, or the germ of an idea for new models, which deserve further elaboration and exploration. Too many of the existing programs are based upon the traditional research-oriented disciplinary Ph.D. and are well-suited neither to the preparation of researchers in the broad supradisciplinary field of higher education nor to the production of practitioners in some aspect of the field. We believe that imaginative and innovative models can and should be developed and appraised.

Chapter Six

PROSPECTS AND NEEDS

Previous chapters have already indicated some major issues in defining higher education programs and the disagreements, ambiguities, and doubts within and among programs as to how these issues should be resolved. Many of the programs are new and the faculty are still seeking a definitive role in them both within the university and outside. The inclusive nature of the term *higher education,* itself, and the changing nature of the higher education enterprise—growth of technical institutes and community colleges, involvement of basic disciplines in studies of higher education, the development of the Doctor of Arts degree, the changing structures of governance both internally and externally, and stringencies in financial support—complicate and confuse the scene. The new and developing program does not have as yet sufficient history to define the more successful roles nor the long existing and respected status which permits a program to define its own role and and withstand pressures to alter or augment it. Expansion in purposes and program has usually been the route to increased resources, but in recent years—as some departments have found to their sor-

142

row—expansion does not necessarily bring new resources and staff
to meet the new obligations.

Are Higher Education Programs Needed?

Despite the involvement of both authors in programs of
higher education, our original commitment to cooperate in this
study was stimulated, in part, by doubts as to whether such programs were actually needed. Universities tend to proliferate specialties based more on ego needs and interests of faculty than on
well-documented social needs and statement of purposes. Could the
emergence of higher education programs be only another example?
In expressing our doubts, we were not really questioning the value
of courses about higher education, for higher education has become
an enterprise of such scope that formal study is certainly appropriate. But most courses dealing with higher education could be provided in existing departments: history of higher education in the
history department, economics of higher education in the economics
department, study of the college student in the psychology or educational psychology department, finance in the college of business.
College teachers have traditionally been prepared in the department
of their major interest; even the new degree, the Doctor of Arts,
holds to the pattern despite its deficiencies as a means of preparing
teachers for the community colleges and for undergraduate programs which may extensively utilize an interdisciplinary approach.
We suspect, though we are not prepared to substantiate it, that the
best research on problems of higher education is done by scholars
originally educated and perhaps mainly recognized in history, economics, sociology, psychology, and evaluation. The most significant
work on undergraduate instruction, curriculum development in the
sciences, social sciences, humanities, and the professions has resulted
from cooperative efforts of specialists in these fields, not from persons with doctorates in education. Service programs for community
colleges, liberal arts colleges, and vocational programs have long
been provided by universities by using interested faculty members
from the disciplines or professional schools. Why, then, do we need
programs in higher education? May we not thereby simply extend
a troublesome dichotomy between education and the substantive

disciplines or professions which has long hampered efforts to improve undergraduate teacher preparation? Is there any evidence that departments and centers for higher education can do a better job or meet a different set of needs than the long existing structure? We are convinced that the answer to both aspects of this question must be "yes," but we still share some uncertainties and concerns about the extent, the nature, and the location in the university structure of such departments and centers. In the remainder of this chapter we shall review our own thinking in arriving at this point of view.

The faculty of the substantive disciplines and professional schools have not generally displayed either interest in or enthusiasm for the preparation of teachers, administrative personnel, or for study in depth of the problems of higher education. Only the established scholar dare turn his attention to these matters, for scholarly reputations are not established in a discipline by attention to these peripheral issues. And the scholar in a discipline who does accept the challenge is isolated from scholars in other disciplines who also turn their attention to the problems of higher education. This isolation is unfortunate, for the major problems of higher education, whether in curriculum, instruction, student personnel, finance, budgetary allocations, governance, administration, coordination, or accountability, are individually not confined to a single or even a few closely related groups of disciplines. Moreover, they are interrelated in many and complicated ways which we perhaps dimly perceive but certainly do not yet fully understand. Many economists, for example, either ignore or discount the social benefits of higher education because these do not yield to their modes of analysis and cannot be assigned a value in dollars.

We suggested earlier that the various courses in higher education be offered in existing departments without adding a new department of higher education. In fact, after having perused the catalogs of most of the universities with doctoral programs in higher education, we found only a few cases in which courses dealing specifically with higher education are offered in the substantive disciplines. The existence of a department of higher education may prejudice the case, but we suspect that had appropriate courses previously existed, either the transfer or the addition of a new department would have been difficult. Courses (for example, in economics or business) which seem appropriate in title and in catalog statements of content for the higher education program may not be. If offered at the graduate level, the course may have several prerequisites. Higher education problems may play only a minor role (a source of data) in the course, which is viewed primarily as an extension, an application of the discipline. Students more broadly interested in higher education may find such courses unrealistic and their grades may suffer in competition with majors. A professor well versed in the concepts and methods of the discipline may be impatient of the possible deficiencies and differing interests of an individual from outside the discipline. To place these comments in a more specific context, the senior author has directed the programs of numerous doctoral students interested in institutional research. Unless a sympathetic professor in accounting, financial administration, economics, philosophy, sociology, or psychology is found, courses selected from these departments may require an undue amount of effort for the benefits attained. It is often more expeditious and more valuable to plan a reading course using carefully selected and highly relevant materials. Rarely in the social sciences is the sequence of topics, concepts, and principles so rigid or even so evident that an intelligent person cannot acquire a satisfactory level of understanding through his own efforts or with the occasional assistance of a professor reasonably conversant with the field. For example, the concepts of cost benefit or cost effectiveness analysis are currently of great interest, though of limited utility, in higher education. One might take numerous courses in cost accounting and in economics without being much the wiser about how to apply them to higher education where the products or benefits are unclear and costs can vary widely with the methodology used. In fact, courses in cost accounting as treated in a department of accounting have limited relevance to students of higher education. And most of the writings of economists on cost benefit analysis are more theoretical than practical in their treatment.

There is another problem in developing a student program using departmentally-based courses in the several disciplines. Even if these were available, appropriately organized and taught, many doctoral committees (and graduate schools) would be unwilling to approve a program including courses from several departments. Minors or cognates of 12 to 15 hours are common, and interdisciplinary programs drawing on two or three departments on the basis of some unifying theme are often possible, but a program using one, two, or three courses from four, five, or six departments is not acceptable. It would indeed take an exceptional candidate, adviser, and committee to draw up such a program and provide coherence and depth. Perhaps less crucial, but nevertheless very real, is the fact that college and departmental budgets are determined in part, perhaps entirely, by the student credit hours produced. Department chairmen and deans, in this circumstance, may actively discourage programs which give credit hours to other departments while retaining the major burden of program planning and dissertation direction in the home department.

There is also, we believe, in any graduate, research, or service program a need for attaining some minimum critical mass. We have no clear idea of what this must be for programs in higher education, but three or four professors with differing experiences and specialties and ten to twenty fulltime graduate students must surely be the minimum mass to generate and maintain the necessary integration and mutual reinforcement essential to vitality. We do not see how this can happen unless a unit devoted to the study of higher education exists. This is especially true for a viable degree program, but to a somewhat lesser extent it is also true for a research or service program which undertakes to deal with the full panoply of issues faced by higher education and the many types of institutions and programs included in it.

A degree program which includes preparation for administration is a professional or practitioner degree similar in nature to a graduate degree in business, in engineering, or in medicine. In such professional fields, courses from appropriate disciplines may be included in a program, but advanced professional courses apply the concepts and principles from these disciplines to the professional specialty. Higher education administration, viewed in this way, justifies a degree program as much as business, hotel, or hospital administration.

Higher education as a body of knowledge possesses no distinctive approaches, methods, or concepts; it results largely from use of methods and concepts drawn from the disciplines and applied to study of higher education. Persons who pursue the study of higher education frequently have no interest in the disciplines except as they provide concepts or methods useful to the problem under study. Specialists in the disciplines, in contrast, contribute to the accumulating body of knowledge, but they may view higher education only as a source of data for testing hypotheses and theories generated in a broader context. Although the volume of this latter activity is extensive, the contributions are isolated and fragmented. Although the systematic application of the disciplines to the study of higher education appears to have been productive, the results are not easily integrated or unified to provide clear indications for action. Indeed, the disciplinary approach is reminiscent of the blind men describing an elephant. Each does a reasonably adequate job of describing a part, but fails to see that part in proper reference to the whole.

If higher education is regarded as a body of knowledge to which contributions may be made both by scholars of diverse disciplinary backgrounds and by practically-oriented higher education specialists, it is desirable to identify the diverse nature of the possible contributions. Both the prior work experience and original disciplinary training influence the focus of the individual scholar's interests in higher education and the manner in which he explores them. Some scholars seek to use higher education mainly as a ready source of data and problems to which they seek to apply their disciplinary-based speculations. Others seek to explore the limits of their disciplines by first analyzing higher education, and then resynthesizing it into a structure more amenable to disciplinary methodology. Thereby, they hope to push the discipline to its limits in understanding and generalizing about higher education. Some simply seek to amass as much information as possible about higher education, hoping that somehow the accumulated mass of evidence will engender more productive thinking. Others explore ways in which universities (and the higher education enterprise generally) are organized and how they might be more efficiently organized. Thus the range of activity is from sheer data collection and description to theorizing in one direction and problem-solving in another, but the relationship is triangular rather than linear.

Both disciplinary-based researchers and professional problem solvers must be in contact with reality through data and accurate descriptions. The disciplinary-based theory development and testing of its implications to aspects of higher education problems provide the basic knowledge, methodologies, and concepts from which the professional researcher gains his expertise. The professional problem-solver, in contrast, is eclectic in drawing upon disciplines only if they assist him in understanding and solving a problem. As Kellams points out: "There are at least two kinds of professionals. . . . The first is the professional who works in organizations of higher education, that is, persons who practice their profession within the complex organization called a college or a university, or an agency of planning, research or control of systems of higher educational organizations. They practice within higher educational institutions, but they do not practice Higher Education. . . . In contrast to the professional in Higher Education, there are professionals of Higher Education. They may be called professional educators who take Higher Education as their special field of expertise—professional higher educators, if you will." (1973, 34–35)

Professional higher educators include institutional researchers, policy makers on academic staffs, staff members of coordinating agencies, some college administrators, foundations project directors, staff members on public commissions dealing with higher education, teachers in colleges, and professors of higher education. The professional higher educator claims professional status because of his complex knowledge base of the institution of higher education. He may be granted a degree of autonomy in applying his knowledge base to particular professional ends. Most college administrators are not professional higher educators. Some do not fully understand the institution of higher education. Most of them are constrained by line authority and must make decisions which accord with criteria developed by others. These are often not congruent with criteria developed by the professional educator. This conflict raises doubts about whether higher education as a body of knowledge can ever do more than provide a general background for administrative work.

Programs in higher education which propose to train practitioners of higher education can be regarded as professional schools analogous to schools of business, medicine, and hospital administration. In any professional school there is difficulty in relating the basic disciplines (those from which knowledge, tools, models and methodology are drawn) and clinical disciplines or fields. The latter require this knowledge, add to it knowledge specific to and derived from practice, and apply it to fulfill the professional responsibilities. Research is necessary to improve practice as well as to increase basic knowledge, but few persons in a professional school are capable of performing all the roles required. Research and teaching in basic disciplines are frequently separated from research and teaching in the clinical or applied fields. And the experience in actual practice (an internship) may require still a different type of faculty mentor —one who is himself heavily involved in practice. Practicing professionals may be brought to the professional schools, and students can be sent to observe and assist the professional at work. The preceding considerations and observations lead us to believe that three relatively distinctive types of higher education study may be desirable. While most existing programs (see Chapter Two) contain elements of the programs we are about to propose, our models would make clear distinctions in both the objectives and operation of these and future programs, to the benefit of the whole field of higher education and the persons in it.

Three Program Models

Type 1.   A department (or center) seeking to maintain a national, perhaps even international, perspective on the higher education enterprise. Graduate and graduate-professional education would be included in the purview of such a unit. Among the characteristics would be a staff of five to ten persons giving essentially full time to study and research in higher education; offering some doctoral work for selected persons capable of significant interdisciplinary study of higher education; providing a program of study for selected persons ultimately expected to engage in upper echelon leadership or administration in higher education; recruiting of students and placement of graduates on a national or international basis. Many students may work in higher education from a base of graduate study in other disciplines—economics, psychology, and the like.

Staff will be highly selected and composed of established scholars usually with distinguished experience as administrators, leaders, or scholars sufficient to have achieved national recognition and holding doctorates from a number of basic disciplines—not from higher education. Staff members in the program will have knowledge of higher education in one or more other countries and will maintain contact in depth with these programs to provide comparative education experiences for graduate students, to provide a perspective on higher education in the United States, and to interpret and advocate the trial in the United States of innovations developing elsewhere. Programs will emphasize research and scholarly effort—not disdaining the practical or applied, but assuming that sound knowledge and ability to acquire and apply knowledge is essential to sound leadership and administration. Such a program will avoid heavy involvement in consultation both internally and externally, but will occasionally accept involvement when significant and far-reaching issues are being studied locally, regionally, or nationally. The program will make some effort to involve or accommodate the interests of faculty members in other disciplines and to provide some course or seminar experiences for selected doctoral candidates in other disciplines; organizationally, such a program will be largely, if not entirely, supported as an instructional, research, and graduate unit or department, not assigned to the college of education, but interdisciplinary in nature and scope, perhaps coordinated by a committee responsible to the graduate dean or a dean of a college or division of social science.

Programs of this type and depth need not be numerous; certainly no more than four to six in the nation would be required. Their scope and probable influence would surely entitle them to serious consideration for some continuing federal support.

The possibility of intensive research, of exchange programs and fellowships for scholars and scholarly administrators would justify the designation of these units as Centers or Institutes of Advanced Study and Research in Higher Education. Such centers should be, in great part, supported by external funds, special study subsidies, and project grants.

Type 2.   A second type of program would be smaller in size and more limited in both geographical scope and objectives than Type 1, although it might handle more students. It might focus on formal instruction and internship experiences for prospective liberal arts or community colleges. Its characteristics would be some or all of the following: A small fulltime faculty of two to five persons; extensive use of parttime faculty and administrators offering practically-oriented courses in their particular specialties; practically-oriented students, and many of them working parttime or while on leave from nearby institutions; a program focused on developing on-the-job competencies through internships, apprenticeships, or didactic use of actual work experiences. Faculty would be heavily involved in contacts and consulting with nearby institutions and with supervision of interns working therein; while parttime faculty would supervise some doctoral students, especially those having interests and aspirations associated with a particular area and desirous of an internship experience in it.

Because of the nature of the program and staff, this type of higher education unit may be more vitally involved in the affairs of the institution. Its responsibilities may include inservice experiences for faculty and courses (perhaps minors), for graduate students and teaching assistants in other departments. Both faculty and student research will tend to focus on real issues and problems and may be directed to study of problems in the university or in nearby liberal arts and community colleges. Responsibilities of the department may include the provision of one or two advanced undergraduate courses or seminars open to selected seniors aspiring to a career in higher education; and might also include master's or specialist degrees especially geared to the needs of lower-echelon administration or to professional program personnel preparing to engage in teaching or administration in their specialties.

Such a department may, for convenience, be administered in the college of education, but its role and designation should clearly set it off from those departments or programs primarily devoted to the preparation of teachers, specialists, and administrators for educational levels K-12.

Type 3. A third type of program would have a much less formal structure and might lack identification as a separate department and staff. Courses or seminars on higher education might appear in a number of departments in education or elsewhere in the university. The faculty might be informally identified by their interests and prior experiences in higher education and by their offering within their discipline courses or seminars especially addressed to higher education problems. Professors of education might thus focus especially on college teaching, evaluation, and courses examining the essential philosophical, historical, and psychological facts and factors which give character to American higher education. Higher education might show up as a minor or as a cluster of courses of particular interest to students pursuing graduate study in other disciplines. Some students might pursue a degree in a substantive discipline with special focus on higher education or a degree in education but with a carefully planned interdisciplinary approach. This pattern already exists in some institutions, and it could well be that this should be the most common and perhaps the most desirable. Graduates of such programs would have a less clear association with the *field* of higher education, but could be more broadly prepared for flexible careers in teaching, research, and administration starting from a traditional and recognized base in a discipline (including the several specialties in education) but including sufficient breadth to adapt themselves to other roles.

The type 3 program also has some advantages in staffing and budgeting. There is no need for allocating specific sums and positions for a department; students and professors need not sever their connections with traditional foci of study and thereby become vulnerable to the criticism inevitably leveled at a new and hazily defined field. At the same time, this lack of identification poses a problem in successful interpretation and operation of the program. A coordinator or a sponsoring committee and sufficient institutional formalization to permit identification of the options in catalogs and brochures is probably necessary. Otherwise the departmental domination of graduate study will effectively preclude such an approach.

Functions and Personnel

These three types of programs may emerge more clearly by comparing them in regard to functions performed and the faculty and students involved. The functions of Type 1 programs are to organize and synthesize outputs of disciplinary based research; explore implications and applications of disciplinary concepts, methodology, theories, and models; generate new knowledge about higher education, its problems and operations; train researchers in higher education; train professors of higher education; participate in training of students in Type 2 programs, especially in research seminars or occasional dissertation direction; and develop models for practical application of knowledge about higher education for use by Type 2 programs and other higher education agencies.

Type 2 programs synthesize and apply knowledge developed in Type 1 programs; train professional higher educators (administrators and service personnel); provide consultation service to institutions and involve students in administrative and service (internships) experiences; may prepare teachers for professional or technical programs or for lower-division teaching in community or liberal arts colleges.

Type 3 programs explore and develop implications of disciplines in understanding higher education and train professors to continue this emphasis either in disciplinary departments or in Type 1 programs.

Type 1 faculty are research-oriented—disciplinarians committed to study of higher education; generalists (possibly with disciplinary background, prior administrative experience, and research interests and capability) who have become deeply involved in research. Type 2 faculty are teaching- and practitioner-oriented— professors of higher education (graduates of Type 1 programs); professors in disciplines relevant to understanding higher education (basic sciences); practicing or formerly practicing administrators in higher education. Type 3 faculty are disciplinary-oriented—professors and researchers in a discipline who attract students interested in applying the discipline to higher education.

Type 1 students show a strong disciplinary background; are more interested in problems of higher education than in discipline; may have had limited administrative experience; become researchers and scholars of higher education; may be employed as professors in Type 1 or Type 2 programs. Type 2 students have a background in education or a discipline; possibly secondary or tertiary administrative experience; teachers seeking to move to administrative positions; graduates become practicing professionals in colleges, univer-

sities, coordinating agencies, or government; may have competency
in teaching a discipline at lower division. Type 3 students show a
background in a discipline; expect to remain in the discipline; graduates become teachers and researchers focusing discipline on study
of higher education; may ultimately move to Type 1 programs or
to administration.

The relation of various faculty and administrative specializations to these three types is depicted in Table 2, which presents,
admittedly somewhat crudely, the relationships among professionals
within higher education and professionals in higher education and
the basic disciplines and professional roles.

Cell A represents administrators (or other practicing professionals) whose basic discipline is an essential aspect of their professional work within higher education—that is, they administer a
unit engaged in research, service, and instruction in their own discipline or professional field. Cells A and D include professional administrators within higher education. For those in Cell D, their basic
discipline may have little or no relevance to their administrative
responsibilities. Cells B, D, E (professors from other Type 2 programs or doctoral degree recipients from Type 2 programs) would
be drawn upon to staff higher education programs (Type 2) which
prepare practicing professionals for activities designated in Cells B
and D and perhaps occasionally Cell A. If responsibilities for Cell
A are included in Type 2 programs, some faculty may be drawn
from Cell A (for instruction or internship supervision) as well as
from Cell B (basic disciplines). Cells C and F (Professors from
other Type 1 programs, possibly from Type 2 Programs, and degree
recipients from Type 1 programs) are the sources for faculty in
Type 1 programs which are largely focused on research and the
preparation of researchers. Cells B and C prepare faculty for Type
3 programs, which are made up of discipline based contributors to
the study of higher education.

Relation to Existing Programs

Because most existing programs in higher education include
elements of both Type 1 and Type 2 programs, these models may be
regarded either as suggestive of a mode of analysis of current higher

Table 2.

Orientation Professional	Discipline Based Contributors to Higher Education	Focus on H.E. Functions and Problems
PROFESSIONALS WITHIN HIGHER EDUCATION		
Administrators	A. Professional School Department Chairmen, Deans and Administrators	D. Arts and Science Deans, Vice-President, President
TYPE 2		
Professors	B. Departments and Professional Schools	E. Professors in Department of Higher Education
PROFESSIONALS IN HIGHER EDUCATION TYPE 1		
Researchers	C. Departments and Professional Schools	F. Professors in Centers and Institutes of Higher Education

C Discipline based contributors to knowledge about higher education
A, D Professional administrators in higher education
C, F Faculty for Type 1 Programs in higher education
B, D, E Faculty for Type 2 Programs in higher education
B, C Faculty for Type 3 Programs
Individuals from Cell A may be included in faculty for Type 2 Programs when preparation of administrators or teachers for professional schools is included in higher education degree program.

education programs or as descriptive of a division of responsibility which should emerge. We should like to think that the analytic stage as applied to formulation or review of a program would result in some move toward separation and clarification of functions. Our views on this flow out of the following assumptions suggested by Kellams (1973, 36–37):

Programs of Higher Education need the knowledge generated by the disciplines, but it must be synthesized and organized in useful ways.

New knowledge about Higher Education is needed and it should be generalizable into principles applicable in various areas of Higher Education. The methodology and conceptual tools of the disciplines should be helpful in the generation of this kind of knowledge.

General research findings and principles, teachable bodies of knowledge which provide the complex knowledge base required for professional higher educators.

Programs of Higher Education with small staff cannot adequately meet all of the functions listed above. Hence small programs must delimit in function.

A division of labor between those who produce the knowledge base for professional higher educators and those who organize and convey such a base seems appropriate.

Role models of professional higher educators (research types or practicing types) are needed in programs of Higher Education to promote the social service ideal.

Each program of higher education should identify the client system which its graduates are likely to serve and it should build its curriculum accordingly.

A Type 1 program which might be designated as a center or institute, would be budgeted and staffed for research, although it accepts a few well-prepared, research-minded students. Such a center is really a universitywide department using interested faculty from any discipline, especially the social, political, and behavioral sciences and becomes itself almost a behavioral science department. The students are immersed in a research-oriented operation which provides a socialization process entirely consonant with their career goals. The problems of higher education are ultimately the problems of people and are generated by people. Hence the presence of research-oriented behavioral science disciplinarians is essential. Ideally, institutional researchers would also be prepared in this type of program or possibly in the Type 3 program. In the latter case, they would probably not foresee a career in institutional research, but could readily adapt to it.

Type 2 programs present an entirely different problem. It is not evident that any academic program as currently conceived can prepare administrators. Although administrative decision-making has received extensive attention, much of the research and theorizing has dealt with business operations rather than with colleges and universities. Administration is not a clearly understood procedure; it is both a science and an art. Intuition, ability to achieve rapport and acquire the confidence of associates are at least as important as knowledge. Despite ingenious attempts to develop theories of change and specify the means to effect it, most change in higher education—unless stimulated by special funds or forced by a powerful administrator, board, or external pressure—takes place slowly, hesitantly, and ends up being quite different from what is anticipated. Often, new programs and institutions are initiated (land-grant colleges, community colleges, technical institutes, external degree programs, and so forth) simply because the existing institutions are resistant to change. In brief, it is entirely possible that decision-making in higher education is so unpredictable that formal study of it has little practical value other than the realization that this is indeed the case.

Nevertheless, if these three types of programs were accepted as models and consciously emulated by universities, the structure of programs and the evaluation of individual programs would be much clearer and easier. For instance, Type 2 higher education faculty members could limit themselves entirely to the preparation of practitioners, rather than try to do some research and train some researchers, engage in consultation and inservice activities and involve some of their students in them, and attempt to prepare teachers in disciplines as well as for higher education. Without the current diversification and proliferation, which arises from a tendency to accommodate every demand lest some other university benefit from the refusal, mediocrity would be lessened. The faculty would become less burdened; both faculty scholarship and the students would benefit. This is especially true for a department in which the major function is currently seen as instruction and the time assigned for service and research is inadequate.

A clearer delineation between training of practitioners and conducting of research would also produce atmospheres conducive to each. A faculty which accepts heavy instructional burdens and a service role is likely not to be primarily interested in research, and perhaps, at best, turns out an occasional descriptive or reportorial journal article based on a survey, workshop, questionnaire, dissertation, or consultancy. The instructional and service environment produces continual pressures which simply are not helpful to research. But at the same time, the environment and the socialization process appropriate for researchers is inimical to the preparation of practitioners. With our proposed realigned structure, prospective researchers would receive immersion in an environment where research is being done, and they can participate in planning, carrying out, writing up, and interpreting research. Prospective administrators would be immersed in an environment where administration is going on from day to day. This would not rule out courses, but would mean that courses would deal with and be interspersed with reality.

The fulltime residence requirement is relevant to the researcher; it may be largely a distraction for the practitioner. The prospective researcher needs isolation from distracting influences, a model to emulate and continual feedback as to the success of his emulation. But too much emphasis on the research aspect destroys the practitioner emphasis. Likewise, emphasis on the practitioner role may destroy scholarly research. The residence requirement removes the prospective administrator from the very culture in which he should be immersed and socializes him in a culture inimical to developing a positive self-image as an administrator. Again, the clear division into research-oriented and practitioner-oriented programs would eliminate this confusion.

Scholar Versus Practitioner

Of course, the scholar-practitioner paradox has long been recognized. The scholar views his discipline as his primary concern and applies it to higher education or other fields only to better understand and expand the nature and application of his models and methods. The practitioner is interested in the discipline only as it is relevant to practice; and, in research, only as its findings enable him to improve his practice. Indeed, if he becomes preoccupied with research, he will reject practice just as the researcher who becomes interested in applying his research and encouraging use of it may shift to a practitioner role.

The socialization of practitioners of higher education involves development of a professional orientation which includes specific knowledge and skills drawn from basic disciplines, which will differ with the individual's interests and with his specific practitioner goals: specific knowledge about problems and attempted solutions in his proposed area of expertise as well as their place in higher education; specific skills—evaluation, accounting, counseling, and so forth—in his proposed area of competence and clear expectation of future role and relationship of educational program to it; development of a set of values and attitudes (personal, institutional, and societal) partially through self-analysis and discussion and partially from contacts with professors, peers, and internship supervisors and contacts and creation of a self-image consonant with the emerging role. These standards apply to prospective teachers and researchers, but since traditional doctoral programs favor a model appropriate to this group, the full force of the specifications fall on programs for preparing practitioners, especially those in administrative roles.

The three characteristics of a profession are the social service ideal, the existence of a knowledge base, and a set of skills in applying this knowledge to the area of service. The social service ideal implies social responsibilities and a code of professional ethics requiring self-control in performing the service. In return, society allows the professional a degree of autonomy in carrying out his professional responsibilities.

The autonomy of university professors, in their teaching and research roles, is presumably protected by academic freedom. However, a professor using his higher education course on administration as a pulpit for public and unrestrained criticism of the university administration or board of trustees can easily impose severe strains on academic freedom. The individual in an administrative role is in an even more tenuous position. Academic freedom offers no protection. Refusal to accept or act upon policies and orders emanating from higher levels of authority may win temporary popularity with some groups if the principle at stake is valid, holds public appeal, or accords with faculty or student convictions. Threat of resignation is usually the ultimate weapon and must be used with care.

Compromise is an essential aspect of administration. There are probably few administrators who have not at some time interceded for special consideration for a questionable admission or a faltering student, salving their conscience with the thought that equity, humaneness, or possible benefit to the institution more than balances the deviation, under pressure, from established principles. The higher education administrator is under such pressures from so many sources, and his success so much depends on weighing and balancing these so as to maintain his credibility that it is doubtful that administration can be regarded in any sense as a profession, or that any abstract or theory-based analysis of administrators has direct applicability to specific decision-making. The constraints and the pressures bearing on the administrators make expediency necessary to survival and practically void formulation and strict adherence to policies based on evidence, goals, and on assumptions and rationality. And, in the eyes of many faculty members formal training for administration almost, in itself, disqualifies an individual for any administrative assignment.

The Department of Education at SUNY (Buffalo) admits these difficulties in its printed brochure on "Doctoral Programs in Higher Education" by stating "The Department does not provide training in administrative skills for individuals planning such careers, rather all of its students are expected to achieve a breadth and critical sophistication which will undergird their service in whatever position they hold." Though internships are available, these apparently are viewed as only one of many educational experiences, although no doubt some students regard this as specific training for administration. Unless departments of higher education are prepared to more carefully define and demonstrate the validity of formal training of educational administrators, they would do better to adapt the SUNY (Buffalo) stance which is unequivocal, realistic, and probably as strong a statement as can reasonably be made in terms of our current knowledge and evidence.

Thus, if we are to effectively train practitioners, we must devise programs in which prospective administrators are immersed in an environment closely associated with administrators and decision-making; a variety of administrative styles can be observed, experienced, and critiqued; the reactions of nonadministrators to administrative policies and the decision-making process can be experienced, analyzed, and related to decision-making procedures and also to experience with decision-oriented rather than theory-oriented or conclusion-oriented research; individuals are required to explore the implications of alternative decisions and alternative ways of arriving at decisions as a backgound for examining their own values, those of others, and the conflicts involved, the strengths and weaknesses of their own personal traits in dealing with people and the more appropriate, natural, comfortable, and productive way of approaching issues and resolving them. Specifically, they need to see that the analytical and deliberation procedures used may be as important, if not more important, than the decision reached. We should use as professors and internship mentors individuals who are actively involved in administration and have demonstrated successful and also thoughtful, analytical, informed, and humane approaches to administration. The program should introduce prospective administrators to research, but in a consumer-oriented context with emphasis on decision-oriented research needed to guide institutional and program development; delve into communication processes as a means of information, involvement, and participation in decision making. It should be involved in the interpretation and dissemination of a research in which assumptions and values are dealt with in depth.

We believe such an approach to training could produce superior administrators for small colleges, community colleges, and federal and state agencies related to higher educators. We do not anticipate that administrators for large universities are ever likely to be selected from this group unless after prior successful administrative experience elsewhere, but we believe that higher education units can make a contribution to improvement of administrative practices in such institutions and contribute to its improvements by developing studies, workshops, short-term internships, and materials directed both to administrators and faculty members holding important committee assignments, or otherwise influential in their universities.

Establishing and Evaluating Programs

We are convinced that there is no need for as many programs of higher education as now exist. We do believe it appropriate that every university provide a few courses in higher education, available under some interdisciplinary listing for all doctoral students (whatever their disciplines) who are interested in a career in higher education. We believe that programs with an administrative preparation orientation for community colleges, technical institutes, adult education, liberal arts colleges, and secondary or tertiary university administrative positions in finance and service areas fill a significant educational role. Such programs should be more avowedly practitioner-oriented in programs, probably grant only the Ed.D. and avoid any implication of major scholarly or research efforts. How many such programs can be justified? We have no adequate basis for an answer. Since many would-be administrators will pursue their programs on a parttime basis, program availability within reasonable distance may be a criterion. Yet overemphasis could only abet aspirations of some faculty members in every university to attain a measure of distinction by adding such a program and hence lead to small and weak programs lacking in courses, resources, and faculty necessary for a sound effort.

As for research-oriented centers or institutes, we have already suggested that they should not exceed five or six. At the moment, we have only one or two such university based centers. Indeed, as we see it, there have never been more than three. To be fully effective, such centers should be able to lay out a long-range program of research, employ a few persons on a continuing tenured basis, and hire others from various disciplines and with differing backgrounds as needed for particular studies. The support of such centers is problematical. Few universities, faced with the financial difficulties and the decreasing enrollment trends of the immediate future, are going to support a center to the extent of a half million dollars or more per year. Foundations naturally avoid such commitments, although the Carnegie Corporation support of the Kerr Commission resembles that model in time and scope. The federal government has been an uncertain benefactor, as the Berkeley Center has found, though the National Center on Higher Education Management Systems at WICHE, with long-term generous support from the U.S. Office of Education, as well as other sources, is an example to the contrary. Incidentally, although the impact of NCHEMS is not yet clear, it does provide an example of the need for a continuing focus and involvement of people and institutions if significant advances are to be made in practice as well as on paper.

The following is a set of criteria and principles for the establishment and appraisal of any type of higher education program. These criteria fall into five general categories: purposes and goals; personnel; organization, administration, and finance; program specifications; evaluation.

To determine purposes and program goals, these questions should be asked. What are relative weights or priorities assigned to instruction, research, service? To what extent are the research and service functions to be directed to local institutional problems? To state, regional, national, and international problems? Is the program to be focused on particular problems, types of institutions, or clientele (community colleges, liberal arts colleges)? Is the degree program to train researchers or practitioners? In what fields are practitioners to be trained? If in teaching, is it higher education, teacher education, or disciplines? If in administration, is it community college, college and university, business and finance, student personnel, coordinating board, or government? If in research, is it disciplinary-based, problem-based, or institutional? What are the evidences of need for this program in this particular university?

Choice of personnel should be guided by answers to these questions. What types of faculty are needed in experience and disciplinary background? To what extent shall parttime faculty be used from other departments? What types of students will be sought (age, experience, career goals, parttime, fulltime)? How many students can be effectively handled in the several specialties offered?

Organization, administration, finance should be determined by asking these questions. What is the rationale for departmental, center, or institute designation? How is the program to be related to other departments, colleges, central administration? Is the organization and administration consistent with the purposes and goals? How are students involved in decision making, if at all? What are the sources of funds? How stable are they?

These questions should guide program specifications. What degrees and designated specialties are to be offered? Rationale for each? What are the admission requirements and how are these administered? What are the major program features? Are they flexible or proscriptive? Is the emphasis on accomplishment or requirements? Are credits for independent study and the learnings from practical experiences acceptable? What are the residence requirements? What are the range of courses? Seminars? What are the core requirements in education or in higher education? Cognates? Are internships available? For how long? Where? Is there a stipend? Who provides supervision? What are the research skill requirements (language, statistics, and so forth)? What type of examinations are given? For what purpose? It the environment conducive to professional socialization? Is a dissertation required?

To evaluate the program these questions must be posed. Are there relationships and coordination with other units in university and with similar units in other universities? Are students satisfied with the program, with advising, and especially with internships? Is there a followup of graduates? What is the quality of dissertations? Is the faculty productive in research? What is the range of services? Are consultants used in program review? Are students, faculty, and courses consistent with resources and goals? What are the strengths and weaknesses as assessed by success in attaining goals?

Such questions of criteria could be developed—as a few persons have suggested (Frances, 1972)—into a set of national guidelines. Presumably these could even be developed as a basis for professional accrediting. We are strongly against the latter. There is already a proliferation of accrediting, causing untold costs to universities with no evidence to demonstrate that costs in staff time and in data-processing are balanced by any increase in efficiency or quality. Hence, we urge that every higher education program undertake its own continuing evaluation and further urge university administrators and state coordinating boards to engage in critical review of existing programs and especially of proposed new ones.

Here, as in other fields, a rigorous answer to the question, Is this program really necessary? should more frequently be answered with an unambiguous negative. And we are also convinced that existing small departments could do a better job by self-examination and strict limitation of their efforts to functions and objectives within their capacity.

For an example of how a program in higher education can be evaluated by a team from outside the institution, see "Evaluation of a Developing Program," at the end of this book.

Assumptions for Program Development

Such broad criteria and principles indicate the parameters for programs in higher education. However, still greater specificity seems warranted through development of general guidelines for program development. Such guidelines derive from most of the earlier discussions and are based on several assumptions.

The first assumption is that the doctorate is probably necessary for major administrative posts in colleges and universities or for professors and scholars in programs of higher education. Substantively it can be argued that the doctorate really is unnecessary for such positions. After all, American business operates with most new personnel holding either the master's degree in business administration or bachelor's or master's degrees in engineering or technical subjects. The tasks of collegiate administration appear substantially no different than those of administering a large corporation. However, the status system in higher education seems to dictate a doctoral degree and there appears little likelihood that a reversal in credentialing is likely. Further, since the university is somewhat unique in that it combines hierarchical, collegial, and individual decision-making, an administrator needs to have experienced the university ethos rather intimately if he is to relate successfully to the various campus constituencies. Corson emphasizes this uniqueness when he observes that "For too long colleges and universities have borrowed their governance models from business and public administration. Neither is appropriate for most functions of academic institutions." He then proposes five principles for the reform of university organization which do in aggregate make the case that university administration is unique and may require a uniquely prepared individual (Corson, 1973, 168–69):

1. The university must be recognized as being made up of groups that are each relatively independent of the institution and of each other and that are simultaneously more capable of exercising power over the institution than are the staffs of the corporation, the government bureau, or the foundation.

2. The governance of such a community requires structure and processes that will facilitate the engineering of consensus: such a community cannot be governed with the structure and processes that rely on authoritative command.

3. A community-wide agency (such as the Council of the Princeton Community, the Twin Cities Assembly of the University of Minnesota, or the Senate of the University of New Hampshire) that includes representatives of all seven elements of the membership of the university is needed as a mechanism through which the president and the board can build essential consensus.

4. The authority of the president to lead what is a large and complex enterprise needs to be strengthened and reaffirmed. This redefinition of authority must encompass not only that of the president (and his principal staff) but simultaneously the precise definition of the evolving authority of the faculty, students, and board. The aim of such a redefinition is to authorize the president to make promptly those decisions that are essential to the efficient functioning of the institution while permitting the democratic participation of each constituency in the formulation of institutional policies by which the president will be guided.

5. A system of accountability must be (and gradually is being) established. Such a system constitutes the quid pro quo for (a) the redefinition, enlargement, and affirmation of the president's authority for executive leadership; (b) the freedom of the individual faculty members; and (c) the abandonment of institutional regulations of the social lives of students and the reduction of proscriptions on the academic path that they will follow.

It can reasonably be argued that the experience of earning a doctorate is the best possible way for a person to develop sensitivity to those unique qualities of the institution of higher education. It is also assumed that doctoral programs in higher education will continue to devote most of their educational efforts to preparing administrators. Schools of education are essentially professional schools created and maintained to provide trained manpower for the nation's educational establishments. Programs in higher education are part of that overall mission. It appears that most students attracted to programs aspire to administrative roles rather than scholarly ones, and it also appears that the programs as they have developed are best suited to that purpose. The faculty in Administration and Policy Analysis at Stanford (within which higher education is lodged administratively), after considering the alternatives open to a highly research-oriented faculty, decided the proper emphasis would be 80 percent of students aiming or prepared for administrative roles with only 20 percent prepared for research or scholarly roles. Such a decision, of course, has important curricular implications.

A third assumption is that the rate of absorption of graduates from programs in higher education will decelerate in the future. With higher education, as noted, approaching a steady or even declining state, the creation of new institutions will probably cease by the early 1980s and actual enrollment will probably decline during the 1980s. Incumbents will remain in administrative posts longer and the turnover, of course, will be considerably lighter. While it seems likely that there will be some expansion of the higher education suprainstitutional bureaucracy to absorb some graduates, the expansion of that superstructure will gradually come to a halt. Because there is a great deal of interest in higher education as an institutional phenomena, it would be relatively easy for programs to double or triple their enrollments. However, such a course seems to be unwise.

Another assumption is that for many roles in higher education, a master's degree is sufficient certification. For instance, for foreign nationals who come to the United States briefly to learn about American administrative practices before returning to professional posts at home, a master's degree in higher education seems ideal. Also, as state and federal government have become more intimately involved in higher education, new roles have emerged which do not require a doctorate but call for some understanding of higher education—such as a higher education analyst in a state budget director's office or the staff officer for a congressional sub-committee on higher education. We recognize the historic limitations of a master's degree, but also assume that a master's can be tailored to fit the needs of individuals aspiring to such roles.

Guidelines for Organizing Programs

We assume that staff work and policy analysis will become increasingly important in higher education and that perhaps the majority of higher education students will develop careers outside the main hierarchical structure of presidents, vice-presidents, deans, and the like. The days when the single campus governed by a single board and a single administrative staff was the prevailing mode are gone, probably forever. There are almost a hundred systems of institutions, each with a substantial bureaucracy. There are state policy agencies and increasingly federal policy agencies concerned with higher educational matters. Thus programs should give specific curricular attention to the needs of individuals in policy analysis roles.

These assumptions provide a base for several different guidelines which we believe should govern the organization and the conduct of programs in higher education. The first of these involves degree structure. Most universities maintaining a school of education have struggled with the problem of contriving a doctoral degree suitable to practicing administrators. The typical pattern has been to create an Ed.D. degree, combined in some institutions with a subdoctoral educational specialist degree. However, all too often Ed.D. degree programs have unfortunately regressed toward the form, but generally not the substance, of Ph.D. programs. This regression is obviously caused by the presumed higher regard for the Ph.D., largely due to the hegemony of universities of graduate faculties in arts and sciences. Yet a regressed Ed.D. degree can never exactly compare to the Ph.D. if the presumed needs of practicing administrators are accommodated. The result is that Ed.D. candidates have been forced to overcome hurdles largely irrelevant to their professional futures and to contrive dissertations which resemble Ph.D. theses but for which they have been inadequately prepared. The regression has intensified recently when institutions began to drop certain historical requirements for the Ph.D. Prior to the mid-60s the Ed.D. degree seemed to be in the ascendancy in schools of education, but when the language requirements for the Ph.D. came to be modified or eliminated, almost immediately the popularity of the Ph.D. degree rose among education students. However, most Ph.D. candidates were not prepared to produce dissertations comparable in sophistication to those of their counterparts in the arts and sciences. The products were hybrids possessing some of the characteristics of the Ed.D. candidates and some of the Ph.D. candidates.

One way out of this dilemma, of course, would be to eliminate the Ed.D. degree and to impose requirements for the Ph.D. comparable to those in the graduate schools of arts and sciences. Such an alternative possesses considerable appeal for a disciplinary-prepared faculty, but does not accommodate the interests or needs of the large majority of applicants to schools of education. The opposite alternative of offering only the Ed.D. degree also seems unwise because it would minimize the contributions of the academic or scholarly portion of a faculty and would eliminate any possibility of preparing students for roles in research or as professors of higher education. A compromise would offer both the Ed.D. degree and the Ph.D. degree but make them clearly distinctive. Although there is some basis for the presumed difference in status or prestige between the Ed.D. and the Ph.D. degrees, in education the difference has not been reflected in subsequent professional status or rewards. Thus the task facing a department of higher education is to tailor the Ed.D. degree so that it would be clearly desirable for students aspiring to administrative positions—first by making the Ed.D. the principal degree offered, so that any possible invidious distinction would be offset by the larger number of Ed.D. students; second, by relieving Ed.D. candidates from doing dissertation proposals in the Ph.D. mode, requiring theory and analytical skills which they had not understood, and requiring them instead to synthesize a variety of concepts, theories, and evidence in solving applied problems. (For example, a dissertation examining the admissions policies of the Claremont group of colleges in the light of changing admissions policies nationally, all leading to specific recommendations, would have proven unacceptable as a Ph.D.

thesis. However, such an inquiry well designed and rigorously constructed, should be highly appropriate for an Ed.D. program.) And third, by designing the Ed.D. program to be completed in not more than three years past the master's with an expected mean time of completion in two-and-a-half years after the masters degree. Thus students who opted for the Ph.D. degree would recognize that it probably would require a longer period and would take that option only if they had clearly-focused research goals for themselves.

A carefully contrived Ed.D. degree could also serve as a vehicle for a revitalized master's degree. The first academic year could be the same for individuals seeking a master's or an Ed.D. degree. For the doctoral candidate the second year would consist simply of deepening insight, gaining some supervised internship experience and developing an applied thesis, presumably, which would help in subsequent professional work.

The interim educational specialist degree seems never to have proven satisfactory. It was designed to develop quite technical skills such as those needed for school plant planning, but it always suffered invidiously when compared to the doctorate and seems gradually to have fallen into disuse. There seems no particular reason to suggest a resurrection.

Some departments of higher education have devoted considerable attention to the preparation of persons who aspire to teach in one of the substantive academic fields. Such an effort seems inappropriate. While it seems obvious that Ph.D. programs have not prepared candidates for their roles as teachers, this is not a persuasive argument for creation of a new degree, especially since it seems inevitably to suffer by comparison with the Ph.D. A more sensible solution would be to restructure the Ph.D. to make it more appropriate preparation for teachers. In this connection Spurr argues: "The American Ph.D. program is broad enough to build into it the necessary elements to make it suitable for the preparation of teachers and professionals as well as of research scholars. To a considerable extent we are already doing this. Many departments are now requiring supervised teaching experience for all their doctoral students and this is all to the good. If formal courses in education are thought desirable the department has the option of requiring students to take them. A department has the right to broaden the concept of the dissertation to include expository as well as research treatment of a topic as Dartmouth has done in the field of mathematics. An English department can accept dissertations whose merits lie in the evidence of the creativity they contain as well as the more conventional trappings of scholarship.

"In short, there is no reason why the Ph.D. cannot be offered as a three-to-four year program suitable for turning out research workers, teachers and professionals. The only question is whether the faculties of the individual departments will face up to the multivariant careers of the products of their doctoral programs and build in the necessary flexibility. Parallel doctoral programs with other names are created only to circumvent the nostalgic purist" (Spurr, 1970, 137).

Actual programs of higher education present argument both pro and con for some sort of a core curriculum. On balance if a core of courses is sufficiently broad-based and relevant to any of a number of subconcentrations, the arguments in favor appear more persuasive. A core of courses taken by all students in a program can go far toward developing a common and a rigorous intellectual view of problems in the field. For example, while it is commonly recognized that the later years of a law program need revision, the first year of law school which is prescribed and comparable the country over, does appear to develop student capacity to think, speak and write as lawyers do, contributing not only a potent intellectual dimension but facilitating a distinctive sense of identity. And a core of courses taken by all students can contribute to a feeling of community. Programs which allow students to elect freely from large numbers of courses seemingly contribute to feelings of loneliness and isolation in American universities. When all members of an entering class proceed through commonly required experiences it facilitates acquaintanceship, friendship, and a sense of group cohesiveness. Thirdly, a core of courses provides a valuable mechanism for group counseling and guiding of students, ranging from simple transmission of bureaucratic information to group consideration of anxieties heightened by approaching qualifying or preliminary examinations.

A core should be broadly theoretical rather than narrowly descriptive. Thus it would seem more reasonable to draw more on relevant social and behavioral sciences and appropriate statistical courses than courses descriptive of unique problems of colleges and universities. Obviously each institution will develop its own core in the light of existing faculty talent, but, to illustrate, a core might consist of three year-long courses, in total comprising 75 percent of the first year's work. One year-long course might be an integrated drawing on economics, political science, sociology and, to some extent, social psychology, to examine social scientific foundations to decision making. A second year-long course might be appropriately labeled decision science which would draw heavily on statistical decision theory and uses of computers in planning. A third year-long course would be somewhat more practice oriented and would examine the nature of educational institutions in their social, historical, political and economic context, and how they are organized, governed and administered. Courses more discreetly concerned with such things as student personnel work in higher education or junior college, when offered, would be taken collaterally with the core during the second year.

Internships represent another somewhat controversial issue. In theory internships in administration should provide experiences comparable to a medical internship or to work in a law office for law students. In practice educational internships seem to have been undersupervised, underfunded and to degenerate either to the students doing routine tasks or to the internship being converted into a fulltime job. Generally, however, the case for internships seems sufficiently strong so that they should become an integral part of programs designed for aspiring administrators. An internship should be required for all Ed.D. candidates, should come during the second year, should be remunerated, should be closely supervised both by the host institution and the mentor institution, and should be explicitly related to an ongoing seminar or colloquium. Internship supervision seems so significant that halftime of a faculty member should be devoted to supervision and the seminar for approximately each eight to ten interns.

National Criteria

Increasingly, universities (generally through their schools of education) face the question of whether or not to offer a formal program in higher education leading to a doctoral degree. Such a decision should not be taken lightly if the expectation is to do more than offer a few courses which might be of value to future educational workers. To answer the question, particularly with respect to the creation of programs designed to be national in orientation (although they can be applied with equal propriety to more regional programs), several criteria are suggested.

The first and most important of these is whether the institution is prepared to support with institutional funds a core faculty, which can personify and give cohesion to a program. Excessive reliance on parttime faculty and complete reliance on external funding seems unwise. A decision to develop a good program in higher education would be expensive but, without solid funding, the program will likely remain ephemeral. Moreover, lodging a program in higher education in an institution in which there is no strong scholarly base in the social sciences, business, law and the like, would appear to invite superficiality. Higher education as a field of study is sufficiently complex as to require great strength from a number of fields.

Secondly, the program should not be attempted unless someone of considerable stature both off and on campus can provide leadership, assign cohesion to the program, and attract cooperation with other elements of the university. This point leads directly to the third criterion, which is the relationship of the school of education and its faculty to other portions of the university. For the most part, schools of education have been regarded as somehow inferior intellectually to other graduate departments, and faculty members have been reluctant to cooperate. The sort of program envisioned requires mutual respect between the higher education faculty and other elements of the university which can underlie reciprocal activity. Probably a task of the highest priority for leadership of a given program in higher education is to establish and maintain good working relationships with other parts of the university.

A fourth criterion is that there should be enough students who are qualified who will be fulltime students to give the program an adequate critical mass. Graduate students do educate each other probably to a greater degree than they are educated by the faculty. Obviously some parttime students will be inevitable. Graduate education is costly and students do need financial support. People working in nearby educational institutions legitimately can aspire to graduate study while still working. However, if the majority of matriculated students are parttime, serious question can be raised as to the intellectual adequacy of the program.

The fifth criterion deals with the scholarly and research competency of faculty members. A doctoral program in higher education should not be attempted unless adequate numbers of faculty members who have demonstrated both research competency and competence in directing doctoral level research are available to direct theses. Obviously a former administrator can make major contributions to an Ed.D. candidate who is doing an applied thesis. However, if there are only one or two experienced scholars on a faculty composed largely of formal or present active administrators, the integrity of the program also can be seriously questioned.

A different sort of criterion concerns the market for graduates. The study of higher education appears to be increasingly popular and institutions experience no difficulty in attracting applicants. However, the market for graduates is less stable. How each institution responds to this criterion, of course, will be indigenous to that institution, but it should be considered carefully before decision is made to initiate, expand, or even maintain a program.

The skepticism with which this book was begun has given way to a conviction that doctoral programs in higher education are defensible and feasible, albeit requiring hard work and adequate expenditure of funds. If an institution elects to develop a program in higher education no better general guideline can be posited than the point of view urged by regional accrediting associations on institutions concerning their graduate programs (*Handbook of Accreditation*, 1973, p. 78):

> *The chief functions of graduate work are to develop scholarship, including interpretation, organization, evaluation and application of knowledge, to develop proficiency in the dissemination of knowledge; and to develop competence in creative activity. To prepare and train the students in these objectives requires a major investment in faculty, space, equipment, laboratories and library. Unless an institution has the potential resources to provide these prerequisites a graduate program should not be initiated.*

The acquisition and maintenance of an excellent faculty are continual concerns of the graduate school. Without a faculty which is intensely interested in advancing knowledge a graduate school cannot provide service to the graduate student commensurate with the accepted standard throughout the nation. Also there can be no inhibition or discouragement of the basic philosophy of research, namely free inquiry and expression of ideas, that will enhance the advance of knowledge. Thus, political, cultural, social or religious dogma that stifles or questions the unrestricted privilege of pursuing knowledge or creative activity in all of its aspects and potential cannot be countenanced. While teaching is one of the prime functions of the university, faculty should have sufficient time for scholarship and the conduct of research in order to maintain excellence in their respective fields.

A graduate school is a community of scholars and students. They profit from sharing their experience, ideas and knowledge. Sufficiently high requirements for admission to the graduate school must exist to attract well-qualified students who will be able to fulfill the objectives and goals of graduate work. The program should be flexible enough to accept students interested in any of the several functions of the graduate program, whether there is a high degree of specialization for professional work, but as well as depth for teaching or competence in research.

DOCTORAL DEGREE
PROGRAMS IN
HIGHER EDUCATION

Name of Institution	Degrees with a Specialty in Higher Education	Department, Center, Institute
1. University of Alabama	M.A., Ed.S., Ed.D., Ph.D.	Area of Administration and Higher Education College of Education
2. Arizona State University	Ed.S., Ed.D., Ph.D.	Center for the Study of Higher Education Department of Education, Administration, and Supervision College of Education
3. American University	M.E., Ed.D., Ph.D.	Division of Higher Education Department of Education
4. University of Arkansas	M.Ed., Ed.S., Ed.D.	Higher Education Program Department of Educational Foundations
5. Boston College	Ed.D., Ph.D.	Division of Higher Education Graduate Department of Education
6. Boston University	M.Ed., C.A.G.S., Ed.D.	College of Education Department of Community College and Continuing Education
7. University of California (Berkeley)	Ed.D., Ph.D.	Department of Education Division of Higher Education Junior College Leadership Program Center for Research and Development in Higher Education

178

Institution	Degrees	Program
8. University of California (Los Angeles)	Terminal M.A., Ed.D, Ph.D.	Higher Education: College and University, Community College, and Continuing Education Graduate School of Education
9. Catholic University of America	M.A., Ed.D, Ph.D.	Higher Education Graduate Program School of Education
10. University of Chicago	M.A., C.A.S, Ph.D.	Program in Higher Education Department of Education Division of the Social Sciences
11. Claremont University Center Claremont Graduate School	Ph.D.	Higher Education emphasis available within Education
12. University of Colorado	M.A., M.Ed., Ed.S., Ed.D., Ph.D.	Higher Education Center School of Education
13. Columbia University	M.A. in H.E. and in A.E., Ed.D. and Ph.D., joint degree program in H.E. Finance and Bus. Adm., M.B.A., Ed.D.	Department of Higher and Adult Education Teachers College
14. University of Connecticut	Ph.D.	Department of Higher, Technical, and Adult Education School of Education
15. Cornell University	M.A., M.S., M.A.T., Ed.D., Ph.D.	Extension, Adult, and Higher Education School of Education
16. University of Denver	Ph.D.	Higher Education School of Education Graduate School of Arts and Sciences

Name of Institution	Degrees with a Specialty in Higher Education	Department, Center, Institute
17. East Texas State University	M.A. in Secondary and Higher Education, Ed.D.	Department of Secondary and Higher Education Administration College of Education
18. Florida State University	M.A., M.S., Adv. M.Ed., Ed.D., Ph.D.	Department of Higher Education Division of Educational Management Systems College of Education
19. University of Florida	M.E, M.A.E, Ed.S., Ed.D., Ph.D.	Department of Counseling Department of Foundations Department of Special Education Educational Administration Department of Curriculum and Instruction College of Education Institute of Higher Education (Research and Service)
20. University of Georgia	Ed.D.	Institute of Higher Education (Service, Instruction and Research) College of Education
21. University of Illinois (Urbana-Champaign)	M.A., M.S., M.E., Adv. Cert., Ed.D., Ph.D.	Division of Higher Education Graduate Department of Education
22. Indiana University	M.S.E, Ed.S., Ed.D, Ph.D.	Department of Higher Education Graduate Division School of Education

23.	University of Iowa	M.A., Ed.S., Ph.D.	Division of Social Foundations, Adult Education, Higher Education and Educational Media College of Education
24.	Iowa State University	M.S., Ph.D.	Higher Education College of Education
25.	University of Kansas	Ed.D., Ph.D.	Program in Higher Education Office of Community College Affairs The Graduate School, School of Education
26.	University of Kentucky	M.A. in Education, Ed.D.	Department of Higher and Adult Education College of Education
27.	University of Maryland	M.Ed., Adv. Grad. S., Ed.D., Ph.D.	Graduate School of the College of Education
28.	University of Massachusetts	M.A.T, Ed.D.	Higher Education Center School of Education
29.	Michigan State University	Ed.S., Ph.D.	Department of Administration and Higher Education College of Education
30.	The University of Michigan	M.A., Ed.S., Ed.D., Ph.D.	Center for the Study of Higher Education School of Education
31.	University of Minnesota	M.A., Ed.D., Ph.D.	Higher Education Center College of Education
32.	University of Mississippi	Ed.D., Ph.D.	Department of Higher Education and Student Personnel
33.	University of Missouri (K.C.)	M.A., Ph.D.	Division of Educational Administration College of Education

181

Name of Institution	Degrees with a Specialty in Higher Education	Department, Center, Institute
34. New Mexico State University	M.A., M.A.T., Ed.S., Ed.D., Ph.D.	Department of Educational Administration Graduate School College of Education Division of Interdisciplinary Studies
35. New York University	M.A. (Student Personnel), Ph.D.	Department of Higher Education School of Education Center for Higher Education Research
36. University of North Carolina (Chapel Hill)	M.A.C.T., 2-Yr. Certificate Programs, Ed.D., Ph.D.	Higher Education School of Education
37. University of North Dakota	Ed.D.	Center for Teaching and Learning
38. North Texas State University	Ed.D., Ph.D.	Division of Higher Education College of Education
39. Ohio State University	Ed.S., Ph.D.	Educational Administration College of Education
40. Oklahoma State University	M.S., Ed.S., Ed.D., Ph.D.	Department of Education Center for Educational Administration College of Education
41. University of Oklahoma	Prof. Cert., Ed.D., Ph.D.	Center for Studies in Higher Education College of Education

	University	Degree	Department
42.	University of Oregon	Ph.D.	Department of Higher Education College of Education
43.	George Peabody College for Teachers	Ph.D. (College and University Administration)	Department of Education Program in Higher Education
44.	Pennsylvania State University	M.Ed., D.Ed., Ph.D.	Higher Education Section Division of Educational Policy Studies College of Education Center for the Study of Higher Education
45.	University of Pittsburgh	M.A., Ed.D., Ph.D.	Department of Higher Education (includes Institute of Higher Education) School of Education
46.	University of Southern California	M.S. in Education, Adv. M.Ed., Ed.D., Ph.D.	Department of Higher Education School of Education
47.	Southern Illinois University	M.S., Ph.D.	Higher Education College of Education
48.	St. Louis University	M.A., Ph.D.	Division of Higher Education Department of Education
49.	State University of New York at Buffalo	Ed.D., Ph.D.	Department of Higher Education Faculty of Educational Studies, Graduate School
50.	Stanford University	Ed.D., Ph.D.	Higher Education Administration Programs in Organization Studies and Administration School of Education

Name of Institution	Degrees with a Specialty in Higher Education	Department, Center, Institute
51. Syracuse University	M.A., C.A.S., Ed.D., Ph.D.	Higher Education School of Education
52. Temple University	M.Ed. and Ed.D. in Educational Administration	Department of Educational Administration College of Education
53. University of Tennessee	M.S., Ed.D.*	Adult Education Department of Continuing and Higher Education
54. Texas A & M University	Ph.D.	Department of Educational Administration College of Education
55. Texas Tech. University	Ed.D.	Junior College Area of Higher Education Center College of Education
56. University of Toledo	M.A., Ed.D., Ph.D.	Department of Higher Education Division of Educational Leadership Development College of Education Center for Study of Higher Education (Research and Service)
57. University of Utah	Ph.D.	Department of Educational Administration Graduate School of Education

* Not specifically in Higher Education but Higher Education emphasis may be attained with degree elsewhere—for example, Educational Psychology, Teacher Education.

184

58. University of Virginia	D.A.G.S., Ph.D.	Center for Higher Education School of Education
59. Virginia Polytechnic Institute and State University	C.A.G.S., Ed.D.	Division of Administrative and Educational Services College of Education
60. University of Washington	M.A., M.Ed., Ed.D., Ph.D.	Programs in Higher Education College of Education Center for Development of Community College Education (Division of College of Education)
61. George Washington University	M.A. in Education, Ed.S., Ed.D.	Higher Education Degree Programs
62. Washington State University	M.A., M.Ed., Ed.D., Ph.D.	Higher Education Community College Education College of Education
63. Wayne State University	Ed.D., Ph.D.	Department of Higher Education College of Education
64. Western Michigan University	Ed.D.	Department of Educational Leadership College of Education
65. College of William and Mary (Williamsburg)	M.A. in Education, Adv. Cert., Ed.D.	Graduate Programs in Higher Education Administration School of Education
66. University of Wisconsin (Madison)	M.S. in Education, Ed.S., Ph.D.	Department of Educational Administration School of Education
67. West Virginia University	Ed.D.	Educational Administration Division of Education College of Human Resources and Education

185

Evaluation of a
Developing Program

The following material is an edited report of an evaluation team (consisting of Lewis Mayhew and two other people) which was requested to review a doctoral program in higher education at a critical stage in its development. The report illustrates the type of appraisal which all programs in higher education might well undergo. Since the original document was a confidential report submitted to the dean of the graduate school, all identification of the institution has been deleted.

We have examined a number of documents and consulted with many persons concerning the Ph.D. degree program in higher education. We are impressed with the strength and the promise of this program.

The faculty has articulated clear and reasonable purposes and objectives for identifying, developing, and preparing doctoral students for work in higher education. In the past, these purposes were focused on the development of educational leadership within the immediate geographic region. The faculty now aspires to national and even international recruitment and placement of students. We believe this aspiration is appropriate and should be encouraged, particularly if the university develops, as seems likely,

186

into a comprehensive university, responding to national as well as local responsibilities. We believe that with the present strength of the faculty and the potential for the future, this program can become one of the ten to fifteen outstanding doctoral programs in higher education.

We find a variety of strengths worthy of comment. The five full-time faculty members are well trained, represent a variety of points of view and disciplines, work well together, and seem to have a collective vision of future objectives. We judge the disciplinary preparation of members of the faculty to be a special strength, not only for the program itself but for the sensitive task of forming close relationships with other elements of the university. The faculty members already have conscientiously cultivated individual faculty and administrative relationships in the rest of the university and are widely and highly regarded. Although program ties with other units of the university are still modest, the fact that they exist at all is evidence of progress in the development of rapport throughout the institution.

We are impressed by the research and service of faculty members, both nationally and locally. The faculty members are in demand over the country for consultation, conferences, and studies. The publication record is impressive and research interests catholic. However, this has not limited faculty members' local service as evidenced by joint appointments with the allied health sciences and psychology.

As further evidence of strength, we note the definite efforts to plan carefully for the future. The faculty was preoccupied two years ago with curricular developments and recruitment of two faculty members. During this academic year the faculty began to plan such new developments as an undergraduate course and possible future expansion of the graduate program.

Sensitive to the need for curricular revision, the faculty has developed a new curriculum. Although obviously far from perfect, it reflects good contemporary thought about what such programs should be. The creation of a core of courses with limited credit hour weight is especially to be commended as a device to provide for common learning and to facilitate flexibility for subsequent program preparation. The possibilities for program flexibility are considerable, and this extends to a concerted effort on the part of the faculty to break the lock-step of orthodox dissertation preparation.

There appears to be a conscientious and concerted effort to upgrade the level of academic aptitude and promise of students recruited into the program, and this effort apparently is succeeding. The number of applications is increasing, and the faculty is maintaining consistently high standards of selection. Their diagnostic examining procedures and the advising system, if it can be manned adequately, should make this program somewhat distinctive.

Because the admission and academic program is in transition, a double standard for instruction, advising, and examination has developed, causing some loss in student morale and surely some bureaucratic problems. We are convinced that the faculty is working zealously to minimize inconveniences, but the fact that the double standard exists must be mentioned if only to strengthen the faculty's resolve to serve their students effectively. Lest this comment be misinterpreted, we reiterate our understanding that the problem is a temporary one and one to be anticipated in a program going through radical transition.

We are pleased to find evidence of strong administrative support and high administrative regard for the potential of this program. The fact that the Department of Higher Education was one of the first departments selected to undergo this process of evaluation is one piece of evidence. Another was the many expressions of high professional regard we heard for individuals serving in the program.

We were especially impressed that on a rainy Saturday afternoon twenty-four students came from as far as seventy miles away to spend two hours sharing with the evaluation committee their ideas and hopes for the program. While students obviously would be (and were) critical about some parts of the program, the overall attitude of the group of students interviewed was favorable, supportive, and appreciative of the very real progress which has been made during the past two years in curriculum development, improvements in procedures, and the like.

We have the distinct impression that there has been a steady improvement in library holdings, and the faculty appears determined to have an adequate collection of the expanding literature in higher education in the university library.

Recommendations

We think that the university should be commended for having initiated this elaborate and costly procedure for evaluation of Ph.D. programs in higher education. We are persuaded that other institutions should follow this model, and we hope that a description and assessment of the process will be widely disseminated.

But no program is perfect, and this program in higher education manifests a number of either real or potential weaknesses. They should be considered, however, in the context of our overall favorable judgment of the program.

1. There is a woeful lack of student financial aid, with only two students holding graduate assistantships. If the higher education program is to follow one of our subsequent recommendations to further increase the proportion of full-time students, the amount of financial aid must be drastically increased. Although the department is not a research and development center and although there is always danger of outside commitment distorting the purpose of the program, we still feel that the absence of any extramural funding must be judged as a serious weakness. Extramural funding could, for example, help rectify the serious lack of student financial support by providing research assistant positions.

2. The faculty is seriously overburdened. Five full-time equivalent faculty members attempt to guide and instruct seventy-some students. In view of the necessity in graduate work to have intense individual consultation, this overburdening is a serious weakness.

3. Currently, there is no consistent placement effort. In the past, this has probably not been important since most of the students were part-time students and already had jobs to which they returned after completion of their doctoral work. However, if the program is to serve a national clientele, problems of placement must be given high priority. Although job opportunities for Ph.D.s are lessening, there will be opportunities for graduates of high quality

programs such as the one this department aspires to develop. Nevertheless, locating positions will require greater placement effort than was formerly necessary.

4. Although we applaud the plans of the faculty to require an internship experience from all students who have not had relevant work experience, we sense weakness in the current implementation of the internship program. Not enough use has been made of internship opportunities within the university, and there has been a lack of administrative effort to ensure that all students are appropriately placed in internship positions. Another facet is the matter of supervision, and a third aspect is the problem of how to keep internships from degenerating into slave labor when they should be one of the richest experiences students have.

5. We understand and generally support the idea of a two-semester residence requirement. However, we found that the students did not regard the residence period as a particularly stimulating time in their professional development. It is our conviction that the residence time should be made intellectually so demanding and rewarding that students would wish an extension of the time rather than a diminution of it.

6. We understand that there are plans for new facilities sometime in the future, but we cannot forego the opportunity to comment on the generally inadequate physical space assigned to this department. The offices and meeting spaces were small and not particularly attractive.

7. We advance this next observation with considerable uneasiness. It may be based on faulty impressions. We found the group of students with whom we talked for over two hours quite heterogeneous in respect to intellectual power, curiosity, and verbal facility. This may only reflect the transition period, but we would like to caution the faculty to provide, even more than they obviously have, many and varied experiences for discussing and writing about intellectually potent subjects.

8. One curricular matter containing two principal facets should be examined. While opportunities for flexibility are clearly present in the program, we feel that inadequate attention is being paid to the development of appropriate skills of inquiry, whether these be mathematical, sociological, psychological, or historical. We

are also concerned lest not enough formal attention be paid to the various and conflicting value orientations existent in higher education. If students enroll in many practically oriented courses, they may lose sight of the values upon which they must base their subsequent professional lives and practice.

We now turn to a number of unresolved issues about which we are reluctant to make specific recommendations. But we wish to stress the significance of these as the university and the department plot their course for the years ahead. Perhaps the central issue underlying all others is to establish a clear and distinctive identity for the program and thereby avoid that tendency aptly described as "being all things to all people."

The first of these is the problem which all programs in higher education must examine: the potential for a saturation of the market for graduates of such programs. This is a rapidly growing field, and we are persuaded that many institutions are entering it without cause. The net result could be an overabundance of individuals who have received a Ph.D. or Ed.D. degree in higher education, with the very real possibility of an academic Gresham's law operating. We believe the faculty should pay careful attention to emerging market trends as they decide on lines for increase in enrollment and productivity.

A second and particularly vexing issue—vexing because of its high national importance—is the relationship of a department of higher education in a major university to the entire junior college movement. Clearly, this rapidly expanding field of education requires whole cadres of new administrative and teaching personnel. It would be possible for a department of higher education to focus upon preparing workers in junior college education, or it would be possible for the various institutions within a state or region to divide up responsibility for this segment of higher education. Our suggestion is that this matter be carefully reviewed, possibly in close consultation with other departments of higher education within the state, so that the needs for junior college personnel can be met while universities also pursue their own destinies.

A third critical issue involves the potential role of the program in the preparation of teachers in the disciplines for senior colleges and universities. Clearly there is an opportunity to enter this area although in direct competition with Doctor of Arts and variant Ph.D. programs aimed at preparing college teachers. However, to the extent that the Department of Higher Education uses its resources for the preparation of teachers (including the supervision of cadet teachers) its resources of time, personnel, and money must be withdrawn from other activities. The present program stresses administrative leadership. The decision to discontinue this emphasis should be made in the light of other demands and other opportunities for the improvement of college teaching. This evaluation committee finds itself either split or undecided on this matter; hence we simply call the issue seriously to your attention.

As the mix of part-time and full-time students is changed, a serious issue arises with respect to the weight which should be put on age and experience in admitting students. Some departments of higher education (such as that at Stanford University) are stressing quite young and inexperienced candidates, while others value experience more highly. A younger, less experienced student population demands an internship program far different from the one needed by a student population possessing considerable practical experience. Similarly, the younger graduating class poses serious difficulties for placement. This committee is not in agreement on this issue, hence we take no stand save to suggest that a decision must be reached.

We support a slow expansion of enrollment, and we also support a definite shift from mostly part-time students to mostly full-time students. We are reluctant to indicate any dates by which a specific enrollment figure should be reached, but we are persuaded that growth is imperative.

We recommend a carefully planned expansion in both enrollment and staff. For example, we would judge that before additional faculty positions are added, a hard money base should be built under any appointments which rest exclusively on extramural funding.

We were impressed with the number of professors elsewhere in the university (in, for example, management, engineering, and policy sciences) who were offering course work and doing advising relevant to the study of higher education. We urge that a thorough inventory of these resources be made and maintained and that the program in higher education make optimum use of them as a means for enriching the program without the necessity of an overexpansion of staff. In a similar vein we can anticipate the enrichment of doctoral programs in other parts of the university through exposure of students to some of the course work and insight of the faculty in higher education. Only after all present faculty resources have been identified and coopted into an expanded conception of the higher education program should consideration be given to the additional faculty resources which may be required.

Even then we caution the faculty not to crystalize prematurely the precise kinds of new faculty strength needed. There were comments that an economist is needed and that a specialist in adult continuing or nonuniversity-based postsecondary education might be added. We have no quarrel with either of these suggestions. We do suggest that all alternatives including existing resources on campus be examined and that the stress be in the future, as it apparently has been in the past, on the strong personal qualifications of the candidate rather than on filling a precisely defined role.

The faculty has rudimentary plans, or at least aspirations, for the creation of a center for the study of higher education. Before this issue is resolved, we urge that a serious analysis of existing and previous centers be undertaken. There is always the danger of a center becoming simply a contract research agency, reliant on uncertain extramural funding for continuity of program. A center however does provide, or at least can provide, magnificent research opportunities for doctoral students. In any event, we urge that a decision not be made lightly.

Other centers which have achieved national prominence have developed characteristic thrusts or interests. Illustrative is the identification of the Institute of Higher Education at Teachers College, Columbia, with liberal arts colleges, during the leadership of Earl J. McGrath. A complex problem now facing the Department of Higher Education is to determine its general thrust and to create a valid and distinctive image since clearly no department should attempt to achieve strength in all directions.

Related to this matter of thrust and image is the problem which all students and departments of higher education face: the definition of the study of higher education. Once the parameters of that domain have been established for the department, there arises the further necessity of interpretation to the rest of the university and to the larger public of the nature of the professional study of higher education and the particular role accepted by the department.

We believe in and have stressed the contribution which the professional study of higher education can make to the better understanding of an institution on the part of its faculty, administration, and student body. We are also aware that there is always the danger that departments of higher education can become simply data-generating agencies for the institution. Thus we would urge that at no time should a development such as lodging a bureau of institutional research within the department be considered. This in no way negates the need for a bureau of institutional research within the comprehensive university organism. It does not mean that cooperation between these efforts is not possible. But it does argue that the central thrust of a department of higher education should be the study and understanding of the phenomenon in the broad sense.

We raise as a complex of several issues the distribution and deployment of resources available to the Department of Higher Education. There is a great deal of interest in an expanding undergraduate program. There is considerable demand for postdoctoral and in-service educational programs, and there is also considerable interest in the idea of a center for the study of higher education. We can provide no definite advice as to how any of these matters should be decided, but we would again stress that entering new arenas, especially in a time of scarce resources, diminishes the effectiveness of other efforts. Hence we advise a very explicit cost-benefit analysis of anticipated courses of action. For example, postdoctoral work in higher education is probably the highest cost per unit form of education which can be offered; external support is hard to come by and always of uncertain duration.

We strongly believe that this department should orient itself to state and national concerns for higher education; that its faculty, as it is enlarged, concern itself with state and national matters; and that recruitment and placement be viewed in a state and national context.

Our last issue is not parallel to the previous points. We are aware that this university, like others across the country, is undergoing serious and possibly agonizing budget readjustment. There may be temptation to impose either an across-the-board cut or cuts which especially penalize small and relatively expensive units. We are persuaded that the Department of Higher Education, although small, should be favored so as to facilitate growth even in a time of overall entrenchment. Our belief in this matter is conditioned by many factors including the potential of major contributions to an entire institutional understanding of its problems through sustained professional study of higher education.

In closing, we wish to comment on the high quality of the documentation which has been provided for our visit. It was clear, complete, yet mercifully brief. We were also impressed with the candor and spirit of cooperation we encountered on the part of every group with which we interacted. We are highly impressed with the potential of this style of program evaluation and analysis. We hope that it will be continued and that it will be emulated elsewhere.

BIBLIOGRAPHY

ALCIATORE, R. T., AND ECKERT, R. E. "Minnesota PhD's Evaluate Their Training." Minneapolis: University of Minnesota, 1968.

ANDERSON, G. L. "The New Breed of Administrator." In G. Kerry Smith (Ed.), *Higher Education Reflects on Itself and on the Larger Society: Current Issues in Higher Education*. Washington, D.C.: Association for Higher Education, 1966.

ARROWSMITH, W. "Innovation and Reform in Graduate Education." *Boston University Journal*, 1969, *XVII* (1 and 2), 30–38.

BECKER, H. S. "The Nature of a Profession." In G. Lester Anderson (Ed.), *Education for the Professions*. The Sixty-first Yearbook of the National Society for the Study of Education. Chicago: University of Chicago Press, 1962.

BELTH, M. *Education as a Discipline*. Boston: Allyn and Bacon, 1965.

BERDAHL, R. O. *Statewide Coordination of Higher Education*. Washington, D.C.: American Council on Education, 1971.

BERELSON, B. *Graduate Education in The United States*. New York: McGraw-Hill, 1960.

BOLMAN, F. DE W. "The Administrator as Leader and Statesman." In G. Kerry Smith (Ed.), *Stress and Campus Response: Current Issues in Higher Education*. San Francisco: Jossey-Bass, 1968.

BRAUNER, C. J. *American Educational Theory*. Englewood Cliffs, New Jersey: Prentice-Hall, 1964.

BROWN, J. W., AND THORNTON, J. W., JR. *College Teaching: Perspectives and Guidelines*. New York: McGraw-Hill, 1963.

BRUBACHER, J. S. "The Theory of Higher Education." *Journal of Higher Education*, 1970, *41* (2), 98–115.

BURNETT, C. W. (Ed.) *The Community Junior College: An Annotated Bibliography.* Columbus, Ohio: College of Education, The Ohio State University, 1968.

BURNETT, C. W. "Higher Education as a Specialized Field of Study: A Review and Interpretation of the Literature." In *Higher Education as a Field of Study.* Proceedings of the First Annual Meeting of the Association of Professors of Higher Education. Chicago, March 5, 1972.

BURNETT, C. W., AND BADGER, F. W. (Eds.) *The Learning Climate in the Liberal Arts College: An Annotated Bibliography.* Charleston, West Virginia: Morris Harvey College, 1970.

BUSWELL, G. T., MC CONNELL, T. R., HEISS, A. M., AND KNOELL, D. M. *Training for Educational Research.* Berkeley: University of California Center for Research and Development in Higher Education, 1966.

CAMPBELL, R. F., AND GREGG, R. T. (Eds.) *Administrative Behavior in Education.* New York: Harper and Row, 1957.

CAPLOW, T., AND MC GEE, R. J. *The Academic Marketplace.* New York: Basic Books, 1958.

CARMICHAEL, O. C. *The Changing Role of Higher Education.* Kappa Delta Pi Lecture Series. New York: Macmillan, 1949.

CARMICHAEL, O. C. *Graduate Education: A Critique and a Program.* New York: Harper, 1961.

CHAMBERS, M. M. *The Colleges and the Courts: The Developing Law of the Student and the College.* Danville, Illinois: The Interstate Printers and Publishers, 1972.

Cooperation in General Education. Washington, D.C.: American Council on Education, 1947.

COREY, J. R., AND MC MICHAEL, J. S. *Using Personalized Instruction in College Courses.* Des Moines, Iowa: Meredith, 1970.

CORSON, J. J. *Governance of Colleges and Universities.* New York: McGraw-Hill, 1960.

CORSON, J. J. "Perspectives on the University Compared with other Institutions." In J. A. Perkins (Ed.), *The University as an Organization.* New York: McGraw-Hill, 1973.

COWLEY, W. H. "Two and a Half Centuries of Institutional Research." In R. G. Axt and H. T. Sprague (Eds.), *College Self Study: Lectures on Institutional Research.* Boulder: Western Interstate Commission for Higher Education, 1959.

CREAGER, J. A. *Goals and Achievements of the ACE Internship Program in Academic Administration*. Washington, D.C.: American Council on Education, Office of Research, 1971.

CREAGER, J. G., AND MURRAY, D. C. (Eds.) *The Use of Modules in College Biology Teaching*. Washington, D.C.: Commission on Undergraduate Education in the Biological Sciences, The American Institute of Biological Sciences, 1971.

CULBERTSON, J. A. "New Perspectives: Implications for Program Change." In J. A. Culbertson and S. P. Hencley (Eds.), *Preparing Administrators: New Perspectives*. Columbus, Ohio: University Council for Educational Administration, 1962.

CULBERTSON, J. A., AND HENCLEY, S. P. *Preparing Administrators: New Perspectives*. Columbus, Ohio: University Council for Educational Administration, 1962.

Current Documents in Higher Education: A Bibliography. Prepared by ERIC Clearinghouse on Higher Education. Washington, D.C.: American Association for Higher Education, 1970.

CURRIE, A. C. "An Investigation and Identification of Higher Education as a Graduate Field of Study and Research." Unpublished doctoral dissertation. Ohio State University, Columbus, 1968.

DIBDEN, A. J. "A Department of Higher Education: Problems and Prospects." *Educational Record*, 1965, *46* (3), 209–216.

The Doctor of Arts Degree. Washington, D.C.: The Council of Graduate Schools in the United States, March 1970.

DRESSEL, P. L., AND DE LISLE, F. H. "The Development of the Educational Specialist in Higher Education." *The North Central Association Quarterly*, 1971, *45* (3), 305–315.

DRESSEL, P. L., AND THOMPSON, M. M. *College Teaching: Improvement by Degrees*. Iowa City, Iowa: American College Testing Program, 1974.

DUNHAM, E. A. *Colleges of the Forgotten Americans: A Profile of State Colleges and Regional Universities*. Carnegie Commission on Higher Education, New York: McGraw-Hill, 1969.

The Economics and Financing of Higher Education in The United States. A compendium of papers submitted to the Joint Economic Committee, Congress of The United States. Washington, D.C.: U.S. Government Printing Office, 1969.

EWING, J. C. "The Development and Current Status of Higher Education as a Field of Graduate Study and Research in American Universities." Unpublished doctoral dissertation. Florida State University, 1963.

EWING, J. C., AND STICKLER, W. H. "Progress in the Development of Higher Education as a Field of Professional Graduate Study and Research." *The Journal of Teacher Education,* 1964, *XV* (4), 397–403.

"Exploratory Development Basic to the Improvement of Preparatory Programs for Higher Education Administrators." Communication from the University Council on Educational Administration at Columbus, Ohio, to member institutions. Columbus, Ohio: May, 1971.

FINCHER, C. "Planning Models and Paradigms in Higher Education." *Journal of Higher Education,* 1972, *43* (9), 754–767.

FINCHER, C. (Guest Ed.) "Higher Education: An Emerging Discipline and the Need for Reform." *Journal of Research and Development in Education,* 1973a, *6* (2), 1–3.

FINCHER, C. Guest Ed. "The Behavioral Sciences as an Interdisciplinary Approach to Higher Education." *Journal of Research and Development in Education,* 1973b, *6* (2), 80–92.

FLEXNER, A. *The American College: A Criticism.* New York: Arno Press and *The New York Times,* 1969.

FLEXNER, A. *Medical Education in the United States and Canada.* Carnegie Foundation for the Advancement of Teaching (New York), 1910.

FLEXNER, A. *Universities American, English, German.* New York: Oxford University Press, 1968.

FRANCES, J. B. "Departmental Development: The Formative Use of National Guidelines." In *Higher Education as a Field of Study.* Proceedings of the First Annual Meeting of the Association of Professors of Higher Education. Chicago, March 5, 1972.

GARRISON, R. H. *Teaching in a Junior College.* Washington, D.C.: American Association of Junior Colleges, 1968.

GLENNY, LYMAN, A. *Anatomy of Public Colleges.* New York: McGraw-Hill, 1959.

GOLDHAMMER, K. *Social Sciences and Preparation of Educational Administrators.* Columbus, Ohio: Division of Educational Administration, University of Alberta and University Council for Educational Administration, 1963.

GROSS, R. F. "The College and University Student Today." In *The Trustee.* Washington, D.C.: Council for the Advancement of Small Colleges, 1970.

GOULD, S. B., AND CROSS, K. P. (Eds.) *Explorations in Non-Traditional Study.* San Francisco: Jossey-Bass, 1972.

Handbook of Accreditation. Oakland, Calif.: Western Association of Schools and Colleges, 1973.

HENDERSON, A. D., et al. *On Higher Education.* Toronto: University of Toronto Press, 1966.

HENDERSON, A. D., et al. *Training University Administrators: A Program Guide.* Paris: UNESCO, 1970.

HIGGINS, A. S. "Reflections of Quality—A Longitudinal Assessment of Doctoral Programs in Education." Unpublished manuscript, 1971. Cited in Collins W. Burnett's paper, "Higher Education as a Specialized Field of Study: A Review and Interpretation of the Literature" in *Higher Education as a Field of Study.* Proceedings of the First Annual Meeting of the Association of Professors of Higher Education. Chicago, March 5, 1972.

Higher Education as a Field of Study. Proceedings of the First Annual Meeting of the Association of Professors of Higher Education. Chicago, March, 1972.

HOFSTADTER, R., AND METZGER, W. P. *The Development of Academic Freedom in the United States.* New York: Columbia University Press, 1955.

HOOPES, R., AND MARSHALL, H. *The Undergraduate in the University.* Stanford, Calif.: Stanford University Press, 1957.

HOULE, C. O. *The Design of Education.* San Francisco: Jossey-Bass, 1972.

HOULE, C. O. *The External Degree.* San Francisco: Jossey-Bass, 1973.

HUTHER, J., AND STRITTER, F. *A Proposal for a New Objective in the Higher Education Program.* Chapel Hill: School of Education, University of North Carolina, 1972.

JACOBS, P. E. *Changing Values in College.* New York: Harper and Row, 1957.

JOHNSON, C. B., AND KATZENMEYER, W. G. (Eds.) *Management Information Systems in Higher Education: The State of the Art.* Durham, North Carolina: Duke University Press, 1969.

KELLAMS, S. E. "Higher Education as a Potential Profession." *Journal of Research and Development in Education,* 1973, *6* (2), 30–41.

KELSEY, R. R. *A. A. H. E. Bibliography in Higher Education.* Twenty-sixth National Conference in Chicago, Illinois, 1971. Washington, D.C.: American Association for Higher Education, 1971.

KELSEY, R. R. *A Bibliography on Higher Education.* Prepared for the American Association for Higher Education, 1969.

KERR, C. *The Uses of the University.* Cambridge, Massachusetts: Harvard University Press, 1963.

KOEN, F., AND ERICKSEN, S. *An Analysis of the Specific Features Which Characterize the More Successful Programs for the Recruitment and Training of College Teachers.* Ann Arbor: Center for Research on Learning and Teaching, University of Michigan, 1967.

LANGE, C. J. "How ERIC Serves Higher Education." *Educational Record,* 1970, *51* (2), 167–170.

"List of Faculty Members Teaching Courses in Higher Education." American Association for Higher Education, 1968 and 1971.

MC INTYRE, K. E. *Selection of Educational Administrators.* Columbus, Ohio: University Council for Educational Administration, 1966.

MARCH, J. G. *Analytical Skills and the University Training of Educational Administrators.* Seventh Annual Walter Cocking Memorial Lecture. Bellingham, Washington, 1973.

MAYHEW, L. B. *The Literature of Higher Education 1971.* San Francisco: Jossey-Bass, 1971.

MAYHEW, L. B. *Reform of Graduate Education.* Atlanta: Southern Regional Education Board, 1972.

MEDSKER, L. L. *The Junior College: Progress and Prospect.* New York: McGraw-Hill, 1960.

MILLETT, J. D. *The Academic Community: An Essay on Organization.* New York: McGraw-Hill, 1962.

MILLETT, J. D. *Financing Higher Education in the United States.* Staff report of the Commission on Financing Higher Education. New York: Columbia University Press, 1952.

NEWMAN, F., AND OTHERS. *Report on Higher Education.* Report to the U.S. Department of Health, Education, and Welfare by an Independent Task Force funded by the Ford Foundation. Washington, D.C.: U.S. Government Printing Office, 1971.

OVERHOLT, W. A. *Higher Education as an Object of Study and a Subject for Teaching and Research in American Universities.* Study initiated in the summer of 1967. Boston: Boston University, n.d.

PALINCHAK, R. S., AND OTHERS. *Survey of Requirements for a Doctoral Program in the Field of Higher Education.* ERIC, ED 041542, HE 001648. New York: Syracuse University, May 1970.

"Plenary Session Endorses Exploratory Development of Higher Education Project." *UCEA Newsletter,* January 1972, *XIII* (2), 5.

Regis College. *Guidelines for Jesuit Education.* 1969.

ROADEN, A. L., AND LARIMORE, D. L. "The Scholar-Practitioner Paradox, Revisited in Higher Education." *Journal of Research and Development in Education*, 1973, *6* (2), 50–62.

ROGERS, J. F. *Higher Education as a Field of Study at the Doctoral Level.* Washington, D.C.: American Association for Higher Education, National Education Association, 1969.

RUDOLPH, F. *The American College and University. A History.* New York: Vintage Books, Random House, 1965.

SAGAN, E. L. "The Emergence of Higher Education as a Field of Study." Unpublished paper. Ohio State University, Feb. 6, 1968.

SANFORD, N. (Ed.) *The American College.* New York: Wiley, 1962.

SANFORD, N. *Where Colleges Fail.* San Francisco: Jossey-Bass, 1967.

SELOVER, N.; TURNER, H.; AND WATTENBARGER, J. L. (Director). *An Evaluation of the Doctoral Program by Its Graduates, 1951–1971.* Gainesville: University of Florida, 1971.

SPURR, S. H. *Academic Degree Structures Innovative Approaches.* New York: McGraw-Hill, 1970.

"The Sweet Simplicity of a Steady State." Annual Report 1972–73. Athens, Georgia: Institute of Higher Education, University of Georgia.

TAYLOR, H. *How to Change Colleges.* New York: Holt, Rinehart and Winston, 1971.

TICKTON, S. *Needed: A Ten-Year College Budget.* Fund for the Advancement of Education (New York), 1966.

University of Virginia. *Regulations and Guidelines.* Center for Higher Education, April 1972.

WALDRON, W. R. "A Survey of Doctoral Programs in Higher Education at Selected American Universities." A summary of findings from a doctoral dissertation. Arizona State University, May 5, 1970.

WALTON, J., AND KUETHE, J. L. (Eds.) *The Discipline of Education.* Madison, Wisconsin: The University of Wisconsin Press, 1963.

WILLIAMS, J. E., AND RICHMAN, C. L. "The Graduate Preparation of the College Professor of Psychology." *American Psychologist,* 1971, *26* (11), 1000–1009.

WILLIAMS, R. L. *Legal Bases of Coordinating Boards of Higher Education in Thirty-Nine States.* Chicago: The Council of State Governments, 1967.

WILSON, L. *The Academic Man.* New York: Oxford University Press, 1942.

WOLFLE, D. *The Home of Science: The Role of the University.* New York: McGraw-Hill, 1972.

WORTHAM, M. "The Case for a Doctor of Arts Degree: A View from Junior College Faculty." *AAUP Bulletin,* 1967, *53* (4), 372–377.

YOUNG, B. B. "The Rise and Development of Instructional Courses in Higher Education." Unpublished doctoral dissertation. School of Education, Stanford University, 1952.

YOUNG, D. P. (Ed.) *Higher Education: The Law and Campus Issues.* Institute of Higher Education and Georgia Center for Continuing Education, University of Georgia, 1973.

YOUNG, D. P. "Legal Considerations in Controlling Student Conduct." School Administration and the Law, Phi Delta Kappa, University of Alabama Chapter, 1972.

INDEX